THEY WERE PRIME PLAYERS IN A BLOODY WAR

LT. COL. MERRITT. A. ("RED MIKE") EDSON—An old China hand, he was a brilliant line officer whose 1st Raider Battalion became the first striking force in the major amphibious attack on the Japanese in the South Pacific.

LT. COL. EVANS F. CARLSON—A military genius and iconoclast, he built the toughest of the tough: the 2nd Raider Battalion, the most democratic and revolutionary unit in the American military. Inspired by Communist Chinese methods of warfare, he marched alongside his soldiers, and fostered the "Gung-ho" cooperative spirit that saved the Solomon Islands—and sank his career.

CAPTAIN JAMES ROOSEVELT—Col. Carlson's executive officer, he was the son of the President: a fighter who asked—and gave—no quarter. He later became commander of the 4th Marine Raider Battalion.

MAJOR GENERAL ALEXANDER VANDEGRIFT—He was skeptical at first about the Raiders' value, but their extraordinary combat victories forced him to change his mind.

SERGEANT ANGUS GOSS—His death on the island of Tulagi proved the tenacity of the Japanese guerrillas—and the bravery of the Marine Raiders. When Japanese defending a cave repelled his grenade and TNT attacks, Goss charged inside, firing his submachine gun. The Raiders who followed him in found Goss dead—along with twelve Japanese.

PRAISE FOR EDWIN P. HOYT'S PREVIOUS MILITARY HISTORIES:

JAPAN'S WAR: The Great Pacific Conflict

"A brilliantly accurate history . . . huge in scope, superbly researched, and eminently readable."

—Library Journal

"A fascinating account . . . an absorbing and intriguing book . . . Hoyt has produced another must for readers."

—The San Diego Union

"A superb job."

—Military Review

THE PUSAN PERIMETER: Korea, 1950

"Painstaking researched . . . a definitive resource for military scholars and war buffs."

—The New York Times Book Review

PACIFIC DESTINY: The Story of America in the Western Sea from the Early 1800s to the 1980s

"Extremely readable . . . written for the educated layman . . . narrative history at its best. Readers will find it carefully written, seriously researched, and always exciting."

—History magazine

THE MARINE RAIDERS

Edwin P. Hoyt

POCKET BOOKS

New York   London   Toronto   Sydney   Tokyo

An *Original* Publication of POCKET BOOKS

POCKET BOOKS, a division of Simon & Schuster Inc.
1230 Avenue of the Americas, New York, NY 10020

Copyright © 1989 by Edwin P. Hoyt
Cover art copyright © 1989 Peter Caras

ISBN: 0-671-66615-0

First Pocket Books printing April 1989

10 9 8 7 6 5 4 3 2 1

POCKET and colophon are trademarks of
Simon & Schuster Inc.

Printed in the U.S.A.

Cast of Characters

Lieutenant Colonel Merritt A. Edson, commander of the 1st Raider Battalion

Lieutenant Colonel Evans Carlson, commander of the 2nd Raider Battalion

Major James Roosevelt, son of FDR and Carlson's executive officer. Later commander of the 4th Marine Raider Battalion

Major General Alexander Vendegrift, commander of the marines on Guadalcanal

Lieutenant Colonel Samuel Griffith. "Red Mike" Edson's executive officer

Major Kenneth Bailey. One of Lieutenant Colonel Edson's staff

Lieutenant General Hitoshi Imamura, commander of Japanese troops in the South Pacific

CAST OF CHARACTERS

Admiral Isoroku Yamamoto, commander of Japanese naval forces in the South Pacific

Brigadier General Kiyotake Kawaguchi, commander of the first Japanese unit to fight on Guadalcanal

Major General Hariyoshi Hyukatake, commander of the Japanese 17th Army in the South Pacific

Vice Admiral William F. Halsey, Commander of Allied South Pacific Forces

Rear Admiral (later Vice Admiral) Richmond Kelly Turner, American amphibious commander

Vice Admiral Frank Jack Fletcher, commander of the Pacific Fleet air task forces at Guadalcanal

Lieutenant Colonel Harry Liversedge, commander of the 3rd Raider Battalion, later commander of the 1st Marine Raider Regiment

D. G. Kennedy, an Australian coastwatcher

Lieutenant Colonel Michael S. Currin, second commander of the 4th Raider Battalion

Colonel Alan Shapley, commander of the 4th Marine Regiment

—1—

Birth of an Idea

The United States Marines were old hands in China, and that fact was important in the creation and training of the Marine Raiders. Marines had gone to Canton in the nineteenth century to preserve order in a region harried by pirates and ridden with revolution. Marines had participated in the defense of the Legation quarter of Peking during the Boxer Rebellion, and thereafter, until the beginning of the Pacific war, the U.S. Marines had maintained a presence in China. In Shanghai they had guarded the International Settlement; in North China they kept the lines of communication open between Tientsin and Peking, and, of course, they guarded the American embassy in Peking, and later when the Chiang Kaishek Nationalist government moved the capital south, in Nanking on the Yangtze River.

The marines knew a lot about China, and they

watched closely as the Japanese sawed off Manchuria and made it into the puppet state of Manchukuo in 1931. For the next six years the Japanese expanded in North China, and Nationalist Generalissimo Chiang Kaishek, staying south, did little to stop them. But in the north, the Chinese Red Army began opposing the Japanese shortly after Mao Zedong and Ju De led the army on its long march west and north to escape the pursuing Nationalist forces, which were bent on the destruction of the communists.

On the face of it, for a ragged band of communist soldiers in tennis shoes, many of them without rifles, and all of them perennially short of ammunition, to try to oppose the most powerful and modern army in Asia seemed foolhardy. The Japanese had tanks, machine guns, and artillery field pieces. Their army was highly disciplined and the Japanese soldier was the toughest fighter in the world, if Tokyo was to be believed. And yet Mao Zedong's army set out to fight and did.

The Japanese at first called the Red soldiers bandits, and they were not far wrong. Many of the divisions had, in fact, been bandit units until they joined up with the communists to escape Chiang Kaishek's campaign to destroy all military opposition in China. But during the Long March, Mao Zedong had developed a new style of guerrilla warfare, epitomized by a poem he wrote to remind the troops:

> The enemy attacks
> We retreat
>
> The enemy pursues
> We retreat

The enemy halts
We attack

The enemy retreats
We pursue.

Mao also developed the technique of deep envelopment, which involved the luring of enemy forces inside areas held by the communists, where the common people were on the side of the Red Army. The people then spied for the communists against the Japanese, and they denied the Japanese any supplies they could withhold.

By 1937, when the Japanese, expanding south, attacked the Nationalist army forces at the Marco Polo bridge near Peking and the war between China and Japan became general, the communists in the north had perfected these techniques. The United States Marines had been watching, and they saw how effective the Red Army style of warfare was in tying up hundreds of thousands of Japanese troops in North China.

One of the most interested observers of the Red Army was a U.S. Marine major named Evans F. Carlson. He had joined the marines as a private at the end of World War I and had worked his way up through the ranks. He had served with the 4th Marine Regiment in Shanghai, and the Legation guard unit in Peking. In 1938 he applied for permission to spend some time with the Chinese Communist 8th Route Army in North China, and the permission was granted by the marines and by the Chinese communists. So Major Carlson joined the 8th Route Army in one of its campaigns of harassment against much larger Japanese units. He marched for miles at night across mountains, fording streams, negotiating narrow trails along rocky mountainsides, marching up and down ravines, and watching always for the approach of the superior enemy forces. He learned Ju De's technique of surrounding a small enemy force and wiping it out, and then retreating hastily to avoid the swift retribution that the Japanese would inevitably launch.

After several weeks with the 8th Route Army, Major Carlson returned to Shanghai and wrote several long reports to the Marine Corps about what he had learned of the Red Army guerrilla techniques. He suggested that such a force, using those guerrilla tactics, could operate successfully behind enemy lines. Meanwhile other U.S. Marine officers were studying other sorts of specialized warfare with their eye on the Japanese.

The Japanese were expert at infiltration, camouflage, and the use of terrain. Their light Nambu machine guns were obviously suited for location in trees, and in the wooded Chinese countryside they set up many ambushes, establishing machine-gun posts that were thoroughly camouflaged and had interlocking fields of fire. Also, the Japanese fast-moving motorcycle troops outflanked regular Chinese infantry time after time.

In the middle of the 1930s the command of the Marine Corps recognized the danger of Japanese aggression and sought ways of combatting it in the future. One of the problems for the marines was going to be the conduct of operations on many small islands where the Japanese could be expected to have intimidated or befriended the natives. Under such circumstances, the marines would have to use special tactics, and they were considering all the options. Out of this came a recognition in Washington that it would be useful to have special forces of highly trained men who could slip ashore on Japanese-held islands, make a raid, and come back with information to guide the navy in its operations.

The big problem of the navy in the late 1930s was the lack of knowledge about Japanese operations. Since World War I, when the Japanese had been granted control of much of the old German Pacific island empire, no one but the Japanese knew what was happening on these islands. Tourists were discouraged, and if they even came to Japan, they were likely to get into trouble by taking what seemed to be innocent pictures. Japanese security was very tight. Foreigners were definitely not welcome in Japan, and even foreign aircraft were forbidden. As the chief officers of the U.S. Marine Corps realized, in wartime it would be much worse, and so new techniques of securing intelligence about the enemy had to be perfected, including raider operations.

Not all the top marines agreed with this concept. General Alexander Vandegrift did not like it. As far as he was concerned, the marines were shock troops and needed no supertroops in their organization.

There was another factor: politics. Major Carlson was not only taken by the Chinese Red Army's fighting structure and tactics, but by the communist philosophy as it related to the Chinese people. He came away from China detesting the Chiang Kaishek government, which was notoriously corrupt even then. But Carlson's views were radical for their time, and not shared by many fellow marine officers. Also, there was a long tradition in the services that officers did not speak out on political matters. So Evans Carlson resigned his commission in the Marine Corps and began stating his views publicly.

All these arguments suddenly became meaningless on December 7, 1941, with the Japanese attack on Pearl Harbor. Evans Carlson rejoined the marines and was promoted to Lieutenant Colonel. He had the ear of President Roosevelt, through personal friendship, and Roosevelt liked the idea of a striking force like the British commandos.

Lieutenant Colonel Merritt A. Edson was one of the most respected young officers in the Marine Corps.

He had served in France in World War I. He had taken aviation training early in the game, and had become a pilot in the Marine Corps aviation arm. He had served in Nicaragua in the pacification efforts of the 1920s and then in China as an observer in the Sino-Japanese War. He had not spent time with the Chinese communists and had a quite different sense of the China war from that of Lieutenant Colonel Carlson.

He had served with distinction in half a dozen posts before World War II, but his particular skill was as a line officer, and it was in this capacity that he would distinguish himself in the Pacific, ending his career as a general officer, having gone through staff and divisional commands.

With these two fine officers to lead the special forces, the call went out for volunteers for the Raider Battalions. Colonel Edson was told that he could have any men that he wanted. This decision particularly angered Brigadier General Vandegrift as a sort of favoritism within the Corps that was supposed to have no favorites.

But in spite of the objections of Vandegrift and

others, Edson did have his pick of men. Not that he made it easy for them. These combat men were to undergo even tougher training than regular marines. They marched long hours, at night and with full pack. They learned survival techniques and all sorts of methods of combat.

By the end of March 1942, Lieutenant Colonel Edson's men had been toughened and trained so that they could sustain themselves behind enemy lines without communication with other American units. The battalion then boarded the U.S.S. *Zeitlin* on April 12, 1942, and set sail for Samoa. Here they would become expert in the tactics of island warfare. They landed at Tutuila and were assigned immediately to reinforce the garrison there. The Americans were expected a Japanese attack at any time, and, in fact, the conquest of Samoa was very high on the Japanese list, just after the conquest of Port Moresby and Papua New Guinea.

Inklings of these plans reached Washington and the desk of Admiral Ernest J. King, the commander of the naval forces. Very quickly King deduced that the Japanese goal in reality was Australia, and that the movement south toward New Guinea and the Solomon Islands was designed to create air bases from which the Japanese could interdict American supply vessels and warships as they came toward the Australian continent. King ordered the establishment of an amphibious assault command at San Diego, and began preparing for a major amphibious attack on the Japanese in the South Pacific. The 1st Marine Raiders, he decided, would be part of that amphibious force.

So Colonel Edson and his men were moved to Noumea, New Caledonia, for further training in amphibious landing techniques. At the same time, Lieutenant Colonel Carlson was training his 2nd Raider Battalion.

Colonel Carlson also went after men with spirit and soon enough he found them. One was Captain James Roosevelt, Carlson's executive officer. He was the son of President Franklin Roosevelt, but that gave him no special position within the U.S. Marine Corps or in the Raider Battalion. Roosevelt might have found himself an easy shore job that would have kept him safe for the duration of the war, but he chose what had to be the most dangerous of all the services, and to boot he now volunteered for the Raiders.

Colonel Carlson had some very specific ideas about training his men, and one was to indoctrinate them with the same sort of democratic spirit as that practiced in the 8th Route Army. There was very little distinction between officers and men, and the slogan of the 2nd Marine Raider Battalion was "gung ho," or, "work together," a slogan borrowed directly from the Chinese communists. In fact, later, when the methods of operation of the battalion became known to the public, this slogan and Carlson's techniques aroused a good deal of criticism in Congress and elsewhere, and some questioned Carlson's loyalties because he used techniques derived from the Chinese communists.

But in the creation of a tightly knit fighting unit, the Carlson techniques worked very well indeed.

Colonel Carlson had one advantage in his training program. He was very tough, physically and mentally, and so was Captain Roosevelt. Both were big men, rangy, with good dispositions but a sharp eye for discipline. Almost immediately under their tutelage, the 2nd Raider Battalion began to take form, just as Edson's 1st Raider Battalion had.

Colonel Carlson was in his forties, but he could outmarch any man in the battalion and often did. And he had one rule: He would never ask any man in the battalion to do anything he would not do himself. Soon enough, every man in the outfit knew it.

—2—
The Gung-ho Spirit

Lieutenant Colonel Carlson began organizing the 2nd Raider Battalion at San Diego in January 1942, just as Lieutenant Colonel Edson was doing across the other side of America. Soon the word was out, this new Raider unit was to be the toughest commando bunch in the world. And among the Raiders, Carlson's battalion was to be the roughest of all.

Anybody who really wanted to know what it was going to be about could consult Carlson's book in the camp library on the Chinese Red Army, which at the time was as close to a Bible for guerrilla warfare as existed in the Western world. Carlson did not want just any hundreds of men, no matter how willing and eager they might be. He knew precisely what he wanted, and as the men came in to volunteer, they were met by the colonel, who had a lecture for them. First he told them how dangerous the job was going to be. That speech was to eliminate the curious but faint of heart. Then he told them that once they joined up, there would be no turning back. That was why, he said, he did not want any family men, men with wives, children, or other dependents. Nor did he want men with special problems. He wanted unencumbered young men. Also, he wanted men who relished hardship, because they were going to get plenty of that.

Soon the word was out around the camp that the Raiders were very very tough, and maybe not so many men wanted to go after all. It was like asking to be killed.

Quite right, said Colonel Carlson, there was a very good chance that a marine was going to get killed on this job, and especially if he did not keep his wits about him every moment. That's why he didn't want anybody with problems.

The negative talk eliminated about half the volunteers right at the start, but there were still far too many men. It wasn't going to be any problem manning the battalion.

For days Evans Carlson did little else but interview. Again and again he told the men how tough it was going to be. And inevitably, every man had to answer one question.

Why did he want to join the Raiders?

Some men said they wanted excitement.

That was the wrong reason and they were dropped. Somebody who wanted excitement was likely to go off half cocked and get many people killed.

Some men said they wanted to fight.

That was the wrong reason. They could fight with a regular marine outfit. They didn't have to join the Raiders to get a fight.

Some men said they wanted to "kill Japs."

That, too, was the wrong reason. Anybody who wanted to kill just to be killing was not somebody Carlson needed. If they wanted to kill "Japs," why did they want to kill them? That was the big question.

All the men who gave these reasons were dropped. What Carlson wanted were men who were going to fight for a cause, just as the Chinese communist troops he had known in China had been fighting for a cause. They had been fighting for the people, for the *laobaixing* of China, the common men, who were exploited by the Japanese. Those Chinese were fighting against oppression, and that was what Carlson's marines would be fighting about. It wasn't because the enemy was Japanese, yellow of skin, and short of stature, but because the Japanese soldiers were perpetuating a system that had to be destroyed so that other men might live in peace.

Carlson wanted his men to understand ideology, the butting up of the American way against the Japanese way, and what it meant in terms of human beings. All the way, from the very first, the men would have big doses of democracy thrown at them. It had worked for the 8th Route Army. Carlson was sure it would work for his Raider Battalion.

Having gotten his men thinking about ideology, Carlson asked the tough questions.

Could the candidate kill a Japanese soldier without getting sick? Would he be willing to fight, march fifty miles, and then fight again without food or water?

That was how it was going to be a lot of the time. It was going to be dirty and rotten and tough all the way, and he did not want any man along who expected any more than that.

These words, usually said while sitting on the ground with the men, smoking and asking questions, eliminated a lot more of the candidates for the 2nd Marine Raider Battalion. Carlson was taking all the glory out of it before they began, and that was just what he intended to do.

In a few weeks Carlson and his officers interviewed three thousand marines, and after the first thousand fell away, awed and overawed by Carlson's hard words, there were still twice as many men as the one thousand who would make up the battalion. They had to find other ways to eliminate men besides the questions. All sorts of tests were invented, and some of them were probably quite unfair. But it had to be done; the number had to be gotten down. And so it was, until the Raider Battalion was formed.

While this was happening, the commander was also setting up a new sort of unit, with much more firepower than the usual marine company.

The mission of the battalion, as specified to Lieutenant Colonel Carlson, was "to engage in hit-and-run tactics, to spearhead amphibious landings, and to operate as guerrillas behind the enemy lines." This mission demanded a much greater amount of knowledge and flexibility than that required of the regular marine. Every Raider had to have multiple skills, and had to be able to manage several weapons. And, as fast-moving fighters, they would have no time to string wires for field telephones, so there would be no field telephones. They would use radio. The platoons would be broken down into squads, as with the regular marine units, but the weaponry would be different. The regular squad consisted of eight riflemen and one BAR man, who carried the Browning automatic rifle, in effect a light machine gun. Since the Raiders needed more firepower, the number of riflemen was reduced and each squad was organized into "fire teams." A team was three men, one with a Garand M-1 rapid-firing rifle, one with a Thompson submachine gun, and one with a BAR. That gave the fire team several times the firepower of a regular squad. In February 1942 Lieutenant Colonel Carlson completed his organization of this Raider Battalion, which was not quite like any other. Carlson had gotten his own way in the matter of changing the unit organization structure, but not without some opposition from Marine Corps headquarters in Washington. As it turned out, the two Raider battalions originally formed were quite different from each other, and in the end this would prove to be a major factor in the ultimate decision about the Raiders that would be made in Washington. Just now Colonel Carlson saw his efforts to change the structure rewarded and he was very pleased. There was a problem about promotions: the corps would not stand for promotions that would represent the fire team system, so several highly qualified men who were fire team leaders were still privates first class and would so remain. But Carlson got around this by his inculcation of team spirit in the men, in the fashion of the Chinese Communist 8th Route Army. He talked over the problems with the men, and they presented a solid front against the brass. The 2nd Marine Raiders were on their way to becoming a highly integrated and very proud fighting unit.

While Carlson struggled with organization and problems relating to higher commands, the men trained at Camp Elliott, California, and learned the new techniques of fighting they would be employing in the field.

All this was done under Major Roosevelt and the company commanders, while Carlson remained quite aloof from the daily problems of training the troops. Then one day they were assembled, a thousand strong, in a field at Camp Elliott, and Lieutenant Colonel Carlson came up in a jeep, led them in singing "The Star-Spangled Banner," and then gave them a talk on what they could expect from this point on. Here Evans Carlson introduced all the troops to the 8th Route Army system: democracy in the ranks. First he invited them to criticize him and the other officers at will. That was how Mao Zedong and Ju De did it, and it had worked, for Carlson had seen it work. Then he told the men that their suggestions on ways of running the battalion would be welcome. This development was completely revolutionary within the American military system, and it was not well regarded by many fine marine officers in other units. Some of them said privately that they thought Carlson was "off his nut," although no one could gainsay Carlson's ability and record in the matter of guerrilla operations.

Thus began the serious training of the most democratic and revolutionary unit in the Marine Corps. The officers lived with the men, and they shared everything with them. There was almost no visible sign of rank other than the emblems of authority. There was no "chicken shit" formality. Saluting was at a minimum and usually reserved for outsiders. When the officers went out of camp they did not go to officers' clubs for entertainment; they stuck with the men. And every officer set out to show his men that they would not be asked to do anything that the officer would not do, from kitchen police work to obstacle courses.

Now the really fine conditioning began. They would

begin hiking, and the goal was the fifty-mile hike with full field pack. They were going to be tough, the toughest outfit in the toughest corps in the world. They were going to get so used to sleeping in the open that they would be uncomfortable sleeping in a soft bed. They would end up as tough as the 8th Route Army men Carlson had lived with back in the 1930s, who had thought little of marching for twenty-four hours without stopping for more than a break, and then fighting the Japanese in a battle, turning around, and marching again.

Carlson explained to the men why they were going to do this: because they had to be as tough as the Japanese. And the Japanese could do just this. Part of a Japanese soldier's training was "hot marches and cold marches." In the hot marches the Japanese soldiers were taken into jungle country, dressed in full field uniform and carrying full pack, and marched fifty miles in the steamy heat. They did this until their commanders were satisfied that they could go the distance, and perhaps only with a ball of rice and a plum pickle or even nothing at all to eat. And then the Japanese unit would be taken to the cold country of Hokkaido or North China and marched and marched and marched through ice and snow, bivouacking in the open without tents and without fires. Early in the 1930s, after the invasion of Manchuria, General Hideki Tojo, then chief of staff of the Kwantung Army, had led a column of Japanese troops across frozen ice and swamp deep into Jehol Province to cut off the Chinese, and his men had averaged marches in the cold of fifty miles a day. The Japanese were tough. The Chinese had learned toughness from them, and the Americans would learn from both. Carlson delved back into his

China memories and told his troops in a series of lectures how the Red Armies did it, how they invoked the friendship of the people by kindness and fairness, and how among themselves the soldiers were welded into a unit. He then talked about America, and American institutions, about the town meeting and the democratic processes, and the way they would be transmitted to his unit. And he told them about the gung-ho spirit of the Chinese and their symbols. Gung ho, he said—work together—would be the slogan of his battalion.

"Gung ho," he shouted at the end.

"Gung ho," shouted back a thousand voices.

The 2nd Raider Battalion had its leader and its spirit, and it was getting ready to go into action.

— 3 —

The First Mission

High in the hills overlooking San Diego, the men of the 2nd Raider Battalion trained. From Camp Elliott they set out on two thirty-five-mile hikes each week, and one seventy-mile overnight hike in which they bivouacked in the open. On the other days of the week life was easier, they had only a ten-mile hike, plus training in unarmed combat, weapons, and marksmanship. Their survival course included judo, the use of the trench knife, the use of throwing knives, boxing, stalking, and silent movement through the bush. They were given more training in the use of the bayonet. They learned to use the new plastic explosives to blow bridges and rail lines. They practiced going without food and with very little water. They learned how to find water, and how to conceal themselves in open country.

Lieutenant Colonel Carlson was their example. He

led the longest hikes, and his pack was always the heaviest in the battalion. He stood in the chow line with the men, and he made his own bed in his quarters. He kept his belongings in his footlocker, and it was always ready for inspection like any other marine's.

After several weeks the battalion came down to the shore. All the Raiders had to learn to swim and pass swimming tests. They had to learn to manage a rubber boat in darkness. They were taken by boat out into the middle of the bay and put into rubber boats; their destination was San Clemente Island, and their mission was to get ashore unobserved and make their way to a rendezvous point.

There was virtually no "leisure time." The enlisted men did not go to the PX for Cokes or to the clubs for beer. They went to forums organized by Colonel Carlson. Major Roosevelt lectured them on world affairs. Colonel Carlson led them in singing the Marine Corps hymn, navy songs, and the song of Carlson's Raiders, which told of their courage and strength to take on any assignment.

> They will sing of the sailor and soldier I know,
> And tell of the deeds that were done.
> But Carlson's Raider's will sing for themselves,
> And know that the battle was won.
> (sung to the tune of "Abdul, the Bul-bul Amir")

Lieutenant Colonel Carlson told them tales of the 8th Route Army, how a handful of Chinese troops held up a whole division of Japanese for weeks. He spoke of the enemy with knowledge and respect. He talked about the dangers to the world posed by fascism and nazism, about Hitler and Mussolini and Tojo. He talked about American foreign policy and ethics. He spoke of the gung-ho spirit and explained its workings in the Chinese Red Army.

Every man was encouraged to speak up, to air his views and to ask questions. At first the call for questions was met by silence, but after a day or so some men began tentatively to take part, and others were encouraged, and soon the forums ended up in lively discussions. Carlson made it a point to bring speakers to address his men. Mrs. Eleanor Roosevelt came. So did Major General Clayton B. Vogel, commandant of the Marine Corps, and Vice Admiral Wilson Brown, commander of the Amphibious Training Command at San Diego. General Vogel told them what was expected of them and Admiral Brown told them what was happening in the amphibious command. Secretary of the Navy Frank Knox came to talk to them. All this attention helped to build the gung-ho spirit that Carlson was always talking about. By April the Raiders had become almost as tough and ready as Lieutenant Colonel Carlson wanted them to be. In mid-month Admiral Brown made an inspection, and Marine General Howland Smith came to take a look at them. They reported to Admiral Chester Nimitz at Pearl Harbor that the Raider Battalion was as nearly ready for action as it could be made at San Diego. What was needed now was training in a tropical island atmosphere, and the Raiders would have to go to Pearl Harbor for that.

Admiral Nimitz reported to Admiral King that the Raiders were just about ready for action. What was he to do with them? As Nimitz could tell, the Raiders had reached a high point of training and morale which could not be sustained unless they went into action very soon. Where could they be employed? Just then, except for intelligence missions, none of which had been planned, there was no front on which the Raiders could be used. The American forces in the Pacific were on the defensive everywhere. It would make no sense to send them to the Philippines because the Americans fighting there, and that included the 4th Marines, were in desperate straits on the fortress island of Corregidor, and in the next months would be forced to surrender.

There was still a little time for decision. The Raiders needed to get to the Pacific isles to train for landing in coral-studded seas. And so the men of the 2nd Raider Battalion were loaded aboard transport ships and sent to Hawaii. There they set up camp and began more training. Carlson went down to Pearl Harbor nearly every day to consult with Admiral Nimitz and his staff. Privately some of the Pacific Fleet officers called the Raiders "Nimitz's army" and publicly many officers wondered what use could be made of these specialists. All sorts of wild schemes were presented, including the "invasion" of Hokkaido, the most northerly Japanese island, and a raid on Wake Island, which had been captured by the Japanese in the opening days of the war.

But in May 1942 Admiral Nimitz suddenly discovered an excellent use for his new Raider Battalion. These shock troops would be sent to Midway Island to defend that advanced submarine base against Japanese assault.

That month Admiral Nimitz's radio intelligence officers had come up with startling information. The Japanese were planning a major attack on Midway and an assault on the Pacific Fleet to try to finish the job begun at Pearl Harbor by Admiral Chuichi Nagumo on December 7, 1941. Admiral Nagumo had raided Pearl Harbor with six carriers. He had decimated the American battle fleet, had caused great damage to the airfields, and destroyed virtually all the land-based aircraft in Hawaii, but he had not sunk a single one of the American carriers and that is what Admiral Yamamoto had wanted him to do. Now the radio intelligence men had discovered, by breaking the Japanese naval code, that the Imperial Navy's Combined Fleet was coming back to finish the job, and was hoping to lure the American carriers out and destroy them. The Americans had to defend Midway; it was vital for morale as well as for an advanced base. So the challenge could not be left unmet. And if the Japanese managed to land troops on Midway, there had to be a powerful ground force to combat them. Thus the Raiders had found themselves a job.

Companies C and D of the 2nd Raider Battalion were shipped to Midway and they arrived there on May 25, less than two weeks before the attack. But when the attack came, the American carriers got all the best of it, and the Japanese did not manage to land a single man on the islands of Midway atoll. The activity of the Raiders was limited to ducking bombs and strafing attacks while the American carrier pilots sank four Japanese carriers and forced the Japanese fleet to retreat across the Pacific.

At the same time the men of Company A and Company B were again training. This time Admiral Nimitz supplied two submarines to the Raiders for special training operations. And after a few lessons they gave an exhibition for Admiral Nimitz. The admiral and some of his staff had come down to the beach on western Oahu to witness a night landing operation. They were quite disappointed when they did not see anything. Apparently Carlson and his Raiders had goofed up. But then, just as the Nimitz staff was getting ready to go back to base, Raiders appeared all around them. They had come up to within fifty yards of the staff officers before they were detected. Had it been an enemy outpost, it would have been wiped out.

That was the convincer. Nimitz decided the Raiders were ready to go, and his staff had a job for them.

At that time Admiral Nimitz and Admiral Raymond Spruance were laying plans for the invasion of the Gilbert Islands as the first step in the "road back across the Pacific." This was to be the first offensive action under the American war plan, and it was to be accomplished as soon as possible, to get the United States off the defensive.

The Gilbert Islands had been captured from Britain at the outset of the war, and no one really knew what the Japanese had done with them since that time. The atoll consisted of several islands, but only two were of any importance: Makin and Tarawa. Makin, the larger island, was considered to be the most important because it housed a seaplane base. But what else was there? And how stout were the Japanese defenses of the Gilberts? Admiral Spruance, now chief of staff to Admiral Nimitz, wanted to know these facts in order to plan for the invasion of the islands. It was precisely the sort of task the Raiders had been trained to do.

Once the invasion threat to Midway had been dealt with, Carlson could begin to plan for the Gilberts raid. First the engineers built a mock-up of Makin Atoll at Barber's Point on the southwest corner of Oahu. Using their two submarines, the Raiders practiced landings on this point. The Pacific Fleet supplied aerial photographs of Makin, showing the various Japanese installations, and these were faithfully duplicated in the mock-up. During the month of July the Raiders trained and made many landings, until they could find those positions in the dark. Early in August Lieutenant Colonel Carlson told Admiral Nimitz that his men were ready, and they could go at any time.

When Carlson appeared at Fleet Headquarters he was given a new dimension for his Gilberts raid. Since the planning began, Admiral King had discovered that the Japanese were building a major air base on Guadalcanal, and he was determined to stop it. Otherwise, the Japanese would be able to dominate the skies over Australia and to interdict by air the shipment of supplies and troops to Australia. A whole division of marines, plus Lieutenant Colonel Edson's 1st Marine Raider Battalion, was to be landed on Guadalcanal to capture that island from the Japanese. Lieutenant Colonel Carlson's Gilberts raid was to be a feint to keep the Japanese off guard about the really serious move into the Solomon Islands that would begin with Guadalcanal. It would be very useful if the Japanese thought the major invasion was coming in the Gilberts. If they thought there were going to be two invasions, that might be even more satisfactory. And so, as the marines in the South Pacific were nearing their objective on Guadalcanal, the two hundred hand-picked men of the 2nd Raider Battalion (two hundred because that was all the men the two submarines assigned for the Gilberts operation could carry) were getting ready to leave Pearl Harbor on this most secret of all assignments.

—4—
Tulagi

The major problem of the Americans in launching any sort of offensive against the Japanese in the summer of 1942 was the shortage of trained troops. Even the marines of that year were not quite up to their usual standards. They had not been under fire since 1918, and in the years between the two world wars there had been little activity to keep them on their toes. In the months since war began, training had been intensified for the marine divisions, but even so, when it came time to invade Guadalcanal, the best trained marine unit was Lieutenant Colonel Merritt A. Edson's 1st Marine Raider Battalion.

The Raiders had continued their training after they arrived in the South Pacific at Noumea, New Caledonia, which would be the headquarters of the South Pacific command. For the next three and a half months they trained hard. So did the 2nd Marine Division, which would be used in the major assault on Guadalcanal while the 1st Marine Raiders attacked Tulagi, the little island across the gulf which had been captured by the Japanese in May and turned into a seaplane base. The Japanese plan had envisaged an air complex down there in the southern Solomons; the seaplane base at Tulagi would provide long-range air intelligence for the Japanese Navy, and the airfield being built on Guadalcanal would be the base for attacks on Australia and Australian shipping, and later air cover for the invasion of New Caledonia and Samoa. The rapid progress of this activity was what had aroused naval commander Admiral King to insist on quick action in the South Pacific, even at a time when General Douglas MacArthur and even Admiral Nimitz's South Pacific commander, Rear Admiral Robert Ghormley, had said that American resources were too slender to launch an attack. But looking at the Japanese invasions of Lae and Salamaua on the coast of New Guinea, and the attempt to capture Port Moresby, which had been delayed by the strategic standoff at the Battle of the Coral Sea, where the Americans lost the carrier *Lexington* and the Japanese lost a light carrier, Admiral King had continued to insist.

So late in July an invasion fleet was assembled from far and near and sent toward Guadalcanal, protected by a large task force built around two American aircraft carriers. King and Nimitz were staking most of the available power of the U.S. Pacific Fleet on the success of this operation to stop the Japanese at Guadalcanal.

The 1st Raider Battalion was carried in four destroyers which had been refitted to transport troops, the

Calhoun, Little, McKean, and *Gregory.* On Sunday, July 27, church services were held aboard the destroyers, and the Raiders were told the objective selected for them by Major General Alexander Vandegrift, the commander of the invasion troops.

That day the four destroyers made rendezvous with the rest of the invasion force, some seventy ships under the command of Rear Admiral Richmond Kelly Turner, who would be the leader of America's amphibious drives across the Pacific. He was as new to his job as the Raiders were to theirs, but he was confident, unlike the air commander, Vice Admiral Frank Jack Fletcher, that the job could be done. Admiral Fletcher was not under Turner's command, although he was ordered by Pacific Fleet Commander Admiral Nimitz to cooperate with Turner.

As the ships sailed steadily toward the Solomon Islands, Colonel Edson met with his officers and studied the plans. The 1st Raider Battalion and the 2nd Battalion of the 5th Marine Regiment would land on the south shore of Tulagi. Other marine units would land on the islands of Gavutu, Tanambogo, and Florida, while the 2nd Marine Division landed on Guadalcanal.

There was not much to Tulagi except beach. The town itself was a one-street village which had been an administrative headquarters for the Australians and a trading post. There was not much to trade except copra, dried coconut meat which was used to make soap. So, before the war, not many people outside Australia had ever heard of Tulagi or Guadalcanal. The world would hear of them now.

It took another week for the convoy to move up from the rendezvous south of the Fiji Islands. Then came D-Day, August 7. The marines were up before dawn, checking their weapons, blacking their hands and faces so that the flash of sun on white skin would not give them away to the enemy. As they neared Tulagi, a cruiser and two destroyers laid down a barrage. In the harbor were nine big Kawanishi four-engined flying boats, the superb long-range observation planes of the Japanese navy. One by one they were destroyed by the guns of the bombardment fleet. One plane almost got into the air but was hit by antiaircraft fire and nosed into the water to sink to the bottom of the bay that would soon become known as "Iron Bottom Bay" because of the number of ships sunk there. Radio Tulagi, the Japanese link with the important naval bases at Truk and Rabaul, began broadcasting the alarm, and continued until a well-placed shell from the cruiser *San Juan* smashed the station.

At eight o'clock that morning of August 7 the boats moved in toward the Tulagi shore. Colonel Edson stayed aboard a destroyer to keep close to his communications. Lieutenant Colonel Sam Griffith led the Raiders in to shore. Before they got there they ran into trouble. One of the major elements of a tropical island is the coral reef that surrounds it, creating smooth harbors inside. But the coral grows up to within a few feet of the surface, as the marines discovered that day. One by one the landing boats grounded on the reef, some of them thirty yards from shore, some of them a hundred yards out. The marines jumped into the waist-deep water and sloshed in toward shore, trying to hold their rifles up high to prevent them from being fouled by saltwater. Some men fell and injured themselves on the sharp coral.

Some lost their weapons and their supplies. But soon they were hitting the beach and ready to fight. But there was no fight just then. The Japanese were holed up, waiting inshore.

At 8:15 the landing on Tulagi was complete. The beachhead was established and ammunition and supplies could start coming in. The 1st Raider Battalion and the 1st Parachute Battalion moved across the white sand beach to the jungle line, cut into the thick brush of the jungle, and started toward the 350-foot-high ridge that runs the length of the island. They crossed over the ridge and swung to the right, while the 5th Marine troops swung to the left. Company B moved into the village of Sasapi on the north shore of the island. There was no opposition. All they saw were the creatures of the jungle, and all they heard were the birds and the crashing of their own movement through the brush. An hour went by and then another. The whole northwest third of the island was now in marine hands, and still there was no sign of the Japanese.

The second and third waves landed. Company A and Company C followed Company B and Company D up the island. Company E stayed on the beach near the destroyers with the job of bringing ashore supplies and taking care of the wounded until they could be put aboard a ship. But there were no wounded. The third hour passed. The marines continued to advance without any opposition.

At 11:20 the skirmish line approached the Chinese settlement at the north end of the island, the largest group of buildings on Tulagi. The Japanese, concealed in the settlement, opened fire with mortars and small arms. Three marines fell, and as a navy doctor came up to help them, he was shot dead by a Japanese rifleman. The marine line stopped. The fire continued. It was coming from buildings near Carpenter's Wharf, and Hill 208 on the right flank of the Raiders.

The Raiders stopped and reorganized, and then began to push forward against Hill 208. They forced the Japanese back, and the Japanese retreated to another high point, Hill 281. They also held a ravine that abutted the hill. By afternoon the line had been settled; the marines held the ground from Carpenter's Wharf to a little house south of the old British residency. The Japanese held Hill 281 and the ravine below it. Here the fighting ended for the day. Colonel Edson came ashore and ordered the men to dig in for the night. He told them to expect night banzai attacks. He estimated that evening that about three hundred Japanese were in front of them. Many of the Japanese were in the trees, their gray-green cotton uniforms blending with the palm fronds and leaves of the deciduous trees. These were the snipers. They waited patiently as the marines advanced, sometimes letting them get in front of their trees or even behind them. Then they would select a target and fire. The technique was very simple and very effective. The Raiders had taken about fifteen percent casualties that afternoon, mostly men shot in the back from the trees.

Lieutenant Colonel Edson warned his men, as darkness came down, that the Japanese were not finished for the day. At 10:30 that night they came, charging the foxhole line of the Raiders and waving samurai swords and firing bayonetted rifles from the hip as they came.

"Tenno heika banzai—May His Majesty the Emperor live ten thousand years," they shouted. "Banzai. You die, marine, you die."

And they charged the line.

The Japanese broke through the foxhole line between Company C and Company A and this cut off Company C from the battalion. The Japanese moved along the ridge, and came up almost to Colonel Edson's command post. There they were stopped by marines with Garand rifles, tommy guns, and Browning automatic rifles. The Japanese were mostly using grenades. Their rifles were primarily for intelligence: they would fire a rifle shot, wait for the flash of American return fire, and then hurl a grenade. Some of them spoke English and they used that language to try to fool the marines. Thus came into being the protective devices the marines would use all through the South Pacific.

Although the Japanese loved baseball and had adopted the American sport as their own, they did not know a lot about American baseball. Therefore, if someone approached a marine foxhole he might yell out: "Who won the last World Series?"

If the other did not answer New York Yankees, then the marine opened fire.

The Japanese banzai charge was stopped, and the enemy were wiped out to the last man. But another group came an hour later, and the same thing happened. Two more times that night the marine line held against determined attack, and two more sets of Japanese warriors went to join their ancestors.

The hero of the night's attacks was PFC John Ahrens, a Browning automatic rifleman. He held his foxhole against each of the four attacks, firing as the enemy came, never letting the enemy through. The next morning they found him in the foxhole, mortally wounded. Around him were the bodies of a Japanese lieutenant, a Japanese sergeant, and thirteen Japanese soldiers. Ahrens had three bayonet wounds in his chest, but the Japanese sergeant who had wielded the bayonet was dead.

On the morning of August 8 the marines began their attack again. The going was tough. The Japanese had taken over the old British cricket field, and had dug caves and tunnels in the limestone cliffs, giving fields of fire that covered the whole playing field. The Americans were on three sides of the field. They began firing on these concealed positions with mortars and machine guns. The mortars were most effective, and they were in use all day long. It soon became apparent that the Japanese were a stubborn enemy. They did not give up. When surrounded they fired almost to the last, and then killed themselves with a rifle bullet or a grenade rather than be captured. If possible they would kill more marines, too. They would clutch a grenade and run toward a marine, hoping to take him also to death. The marine had to be fast on the draw to shoot the enemy down first.

In the beginning of the Tulagi invasion a marine had observed to Colonel Edson that they were going in without food and without much water. That was right, said the colonel. The Japanese ate food and drank water too, so the Raiders would get their supplies from the enemy.

Now the marines began to see what Edson meant. These positions along the cricket fields were well supplied with food caches and water. The Japanese had planned well for defense.

Defend to the last was the Japanese Army order, and then commit suicide rather than face the disgrace of capture. The Raiders pressed on along the ridge and cornered three Japanese in one hole. The Japanese fired their rifles until they ran out of ammunition. Then one of them pulled out a pistol and began firing that. The marines watched as he stopped, shot one of his companions, then the other, and turned the pistol on himself. When they got to the bodies, they discovered that the pistol was empty. The officer had saved three shells for "the Imperial Way."

Major Kenneth Bailey led a group of Raiders to attack one strong cave. The Japanese had installed a squad of riflemen in this cave, on the edge of the ravine. It was holding up the advance along Hill 281. Major Bailey crawled up on top of the cave and tried to kick a hole through the ceiling, but it was too strong. He moved down the side, and tried to kick away the rocks at the entrance. But the Japanese kept firing through that entrance, and he could not get close enough. He kicked away. A Japanese rifleman stuck his head and rifle out of the entrance. Major Bailey shot him.

This sort of warfare was something new just then. The marines surrounded the Japanese positions, but the Japanese held out stubbornly to the last man. The marines threw grenades into the caves. The Japanese threw them out again. Sergeant Angus Goss held one grenade for three seconds of the ten-second delay period and then threw it. The Japanese inside still managed to heave the grenade out, and it exploded in midair. Goss wired up several sticks of TNT and lit the fuse, then slipped the package inside the cave. The Japanese shoved it out before it exploded. Sergeant Goss then charged into the cave, firing his submachine gun. He died, but when others came in behind him, they found twelve dead Japanese.

Here at Tulagi, on the first and second days, was established the pattern of the island warfare of the South and Central Pacific. The marines had to fight for every foot of ground, every cave. In one cave they found nineteen dead Japanese. In another they found a dozen, or apparently a dozen. Two of the Japanese were still alive, and when the marines came in, the Japanese shot two of them before they were mowed down themselves.

In one cave the marines saw an officer. They brought up a Japanese English interpreter (a nisei) and he asked the Japanese officer to surrender. The reply was a hand grenade.

Some marines were detailed to antisniper patrol. Every tree had to be examined for snipers, and sometimes even then they were not found but remained quiet, letting several marines go by, and then shooting the fifth or six marine. No snipers came down out of their trees. Every one of them had to be shot out. The advance was agonizingly slow as the marines cleared the ground. By the end of the second afternoon, however, they had killed all the Japanese, they thought. The fighting ended that afternoon of August 8 and Colonel Edson declared to General Vandegrift that Tulagi was secured. They had taken one prisoner— only one—and he had been too badly wounded even to pull the pin of a grenade.

So the fighting came to an end on Tulagi, and the marines settled down to clear away the stinking corpses that were rotting in the tropical heat, to search for souvenirs, and to wait for the next step. They did not know it then, but there were still about 150 Japanese alive on the island, holed up and waiting for a chance to die bravely for the emperor and take many many marines with them. Over the next two weeks the Japanese would move around the island, attacking when they could, and killing marines who were so unwary as to be without their weapons. But after those two weeks the island really was quiet, and Tulagi was secure as a base for American vessels.

— 5 —

Makin

The Joint Chiefs of Staff in July had encouraged Admiral Nimitz to begin preparations for the attack on the Gilbert Islands, and less than three weeks later the 2nd Raider Battalion was prepared to go into action in the first stage of that plan.

As the beginning of August approached, Lieutenant Colonel Carlson had only one major worry about the operation. He had ordered outboard motors which would be used to propel the rubber boats into the shore at Makin, and when they arrived and had been tested in training, he discovered that this brand of outboard motor had a tendency to fail when swamped with water because it had no motor cover. He protested to the supply people but was told there was no time to bring in a new order. He would have to live with the outboard motors he had.

The submarines *Argonaut* and *Nautilus* lay in the

Pearl Harbor submarine base on August 8, loaded up with supplies and rubber boats and thirteen officers and 208 men of the 2nd Raider Battalion. The submarines were big boats, nearly four hundred feet long, but they were not built to carry passengers, so the interior was frightfully crowded. Extra bunks had been stuffed into every cranny. Most of the torpedoes were taken ashore to make room for more men, and when the hatches were battened down, the temperature inside the submarine rose above ninety degrees Fahrenheit.

They sailed that day, destination Makin, object reconnaissance. Most of the voyage was made below, with the men lying on their bunks because there was no place else to go. They had ten minutes on deck twice a day, once in the morning and once at night. That lasted for the first eight days of the voyage. But then they came to the point where they were within Japanese air range and the luxury of the few minutes on deck had to be withdrawn on the morning watch. They still got up on deck at night, however.

The *Nautilus* arrived off Makin at three o'clock on the morning of August 16 and waited for the other submarine to come up. The weather turned foul, and Lieutenant Commander W. H. Brockman, Jr., commander of the *Nautilus,* began to worry about the landings and about keeping the submarine from sliding onto the reef. When the *Argonaut* arrived later in the day, Brockman and Lieutenant Commander J. R. Pierce of the *Argonaut* spent much of the rest of the day studying the tidal currents in preparation for the landings.

At 9:15 that night the submarines surfaced and found one another at the rendezvous point. Then they headed in toward the Makin Island shore. The landing point was reached at 2:30 on the morning of August 17, but the weather was most unfavorable, with squalls and strong winds. Should they go ahead with the landing, in view of the conditions? The decision was Lieutenant Colonel Carlson's.

Carlson did not hesitate. He gave the orders and the men began inflating their rubber boats and putting them over the side, then affixing the outboard motors that would propel the boats in to the shore of Butaritari Island.

Just as Lieutenant Colonel Carlson had feared, the outboard motors began to take on water and conk out. The men would have to paddle the boats into shore.

The Raiders were already split into two groups, one company aboard each submarine. Lieutenant Plumley's A Company was to land on one beach and Captain Coyte's B Company was to land on another. They would complete their missions and return to the beaches, prepared to go back to the submarine by nine o'clock on the night of August 17.

But with the high seas, the loss of the outboard motors, and the difficulties of landing in this weather, plus a serious difficulty in communication because of the noise of the wind and water, Carlson decided to land both companies on the same beach and gave the orders. Lieutenant Colonel Carlson's boat drifted away, leaving him stranded aboard the *Nautilus,* but finally a boat came alongside and took him off, and all the boats headed in toward the shore while the two submarines moved out to a point four miles off the coral reef that surrounded the beaches, where the water was deep and safe. There they would await developments.

46

In the darkness, with the submarines moving up and down in the sea and the confusion on the boats, one boat commander, Lieutenant Peatross, did not get the word about the change in plans for the landing, and so this boatload of twelve marines moved on according to the old plan and landed on its original beach. The other seventeen boats headed toward Carlson's beach to carry out the new plan. The failure of the outboards was not as serious a problem—at least at the moment—as it might have been. Foreseeing the possibility, Carlson had made sure that all his marines were expert at paddling rubber boats. So they made their way in steadily toward the shore. The seventeen boats came in through the surf without incident, and the men jumped out and pulled them up on the beach. So far the mission was going almost according to plan.

At five A.M. the marines were ashore, and they were concealing the boats with camouflage netting. There was no sign of action from the Japanese. Apparently the marines had achieved the surprise they wanted. It was true. The Japanese garrison consisted of fewer than fifty soldiers, under the command of Sergeant Kanemitsu. They were on the alert, because the 2nd Marine Division and the 1st Raider Battalion had landed at Guadalcanal the week before and the Japanese were watching every atoll across the Pacific for more landings. But the Japanese garrison was on the lagoon side of Butaritari Island, and the marines had landed on the opposite side. So the Japanese, dug in stoutly on the lagoon side, armed with machine guns, grenades, flamethrowers, mortars, and automatic rifles, still did not know that the Raiders had come.

All went well until just before six o'clock, when one marine accidentally fired his rifle. The sound seemed as loud to Colonel Carlson as the explosion of a battleship gun. Carlson knew then that the shot had to be heard somewhere and that the element of surprise was now lost. He so reported to the submarines offshore, and then he ordered the men to move out on their assigned missions, because it was important that they get going before the Japanese found them. No one knew how many Japanese there were on the island or what weapons they might have.

Carlson sent Lieutenant Plumley and the men of Company A across the island. There, on the lagoon side, was the road. They were to put up a roadblock and stop transportation. As they moved, so did the Japanese, who had heard the stray shot just as Colonel Carlson had feared they would.

So Company A moved out in skirmish style, showing a ragged line that would not give the enemy a natural target. Company B remained just off the beach, waiting to see what would happen.

As the American troops moved across the island, they were met by a band of native Gilbert Islanders, who were friendly. They told the marines that the Japanese troops were concentrated at Ukiangong Point Lake. Carlson radioed the submarines that the Japanese were at the lake, and at On Chong's wharf, which was the landing place for ships. The *Nautilus* laid down a barrage of twenty-four shells with its three-inch deck gun.

Company A's progress across the island, under Lieutenant Plumley, was soon stopped by Japanese fire from machine guns. But they made the road and began moving. They spotted the first machine gun, attacked and killed the Japanese gunners. The Japanese then staged a "banzai charge." Shouting and running, they came at the Americans with rifles and swords. The fire teams opened up with their rifles, tommy guns, and Browning automatic rifles. The superior firepower stopped the Japanese charge and left more than a dozen men dead in the sand.

From the natives the marines learned that there were two Japanese ships about five miles off the island, heading out to sea to avoid the invading troops. Lieutenant Colonel Carlson passed this word to the two submarines, and they tried to open fire on the ships. The problem was that the gunners could not see the ships. Lieutenant Plumley got into position to see them and helped direct the fire. One of the ships he said was a 3,500-ton cargo vessel, an interisland trader. The other was a patrol vessel of about 1,500 tons.

But even with Plumley's help the submarine fire was not effective, until Commander J. M. Haines, who was directing the whole sea operation, sent two men ashore from the *Nautilus* to spot bursts and correct the aim of the gunners. This worked until the Japanese figured out what was happening, and then pinned the two men down on the beach, and the submarines were firing blind once more. But by first ranging on a tree at the edge of the harbor and then traversing, the submarine gunners finally got the range. They put several shells into the cargo ship and set her afire. The crew and about sixty Japanese special landing troops, the equivalent of American marines, abandoned ship and began coming ashore. The submarines switched to fire on the patrol vessel and soon had her dead in the water too.

Soon Lieutenant Plumley reported that the Japanese had four machine guns and two mortars. They also had a flamethrower and some automatic rifles. A number of snipers were concealed in the trees.

Plumley's men moved toward the settlement. They captured Government House, which was the old British seat of government. They took Government Wharf. But then the Japanese held. The firing became intense. One marine stood up to move, and before he could stir, he was hit by five .25-caliber bullets in the right arm and shoulder. Sergeant Thomason moved along the line, encouraging the men.

"Gung ho, Raiders," he was shouting.

The Japanese mounted another banzai charge. But once again the superior Raider firepower made the difference, and the charge was stopped by the heavy fire from Garand rifles, Browning automatic rifles, and Thompson submachine guns.

Sergeant Thomason was hit and fell. It was fire from a sniper, who could not be found up in the palm trees. The firing continued sporadically. Plumley's men then learned how to deal with the snipers: the Japanese had never heard of the Garand automatic rifle; according to their manuals the Americans were armed with the 1903 Springfield bolt-action rifle. After a man pulled the trigger of his Springfield, he would have to eject the shell with the bolt action and then throw another shell into the chamber. This would give a sniper a few seconds to fire a shot. But with the Garand automatic, a whole spray of shells could be fired. The Americans would fire a single shot, the snipers would stick up their heads, and then the Americans would spray them with rifle fire. They killed several snipers this way.

They also learned to strip the fronds from a palm tree with an intense wave of fire, and then shoot the snipers when their gray-green uniforms were exposed.

The Japanese on the ground staged their third banzai charge and once more they were repulsed by superior firepower. Sergeant Kanemitsu radioed his headquarters that his men were dying gloriously in battle, but were dying.

Help for the Japanese was already on the way. Just after ten-thirty in the morning a pair of Japanese reconnaissance planes appeared. They had been sent from another island to investigate. The new arrivals caused the submarines to crash-dive, and they were then out of the land battle. The marines continued to move forward, but the going was harder without artillery support. The Japanese machine guns were very active.

Back on the sea beach at his command post, Lieutenant Colonel Carlson's radiomen tuned in on Radio Makin, which was still operating. They knew then that it would not be long before planes from Jaluit and Mille, island groups about 250 miles away, would be coming over and making problems more difficult.

Carlson was growing nervous. Anything could happen. Any sort of reinforcement might occur. The Raiders were taking too long. He paced along the beach, "smoking that stinking pipe of his," as one Raider put it. He put down the pipe and chain-smoked cigarettes. He went up to the perimeter to see what Plumley and his men were doing. He went back to his command post. There he fidgeted.

As the line was slowed, Carlson ordered a platoon

from Company B to reinforce Plumley, and Lieutenant Griffith led the men forward. The Japanese fired steadily and called out insults. "Roosevelt bastards," they shouted, not knowing how right they were. Major Roosevelt, the son of the President, was right there with Carlson.

"Marine, you die," shouted the Japanese. But it was Japanese who were dying for the most part, as the Raiders moved slowly ahead into the former British colonial settlement.

The Japanese reconnaissance planes circled lazily, and circled again. Then each of them dropped a single bomb in the area where the marines were fighting, and both moved off to the north. They were headed for base, to report and get more help, Carlson knew.

Time went by. About an hour and a half passed. Shortly after 1:30 Carlson heard and then saw what he hated—a dozen Japanese planes headed for the atoll. Four of the planes were Zero fighters. The rest were a mixed bag of bombers, including two big Kawanishi flying boats. For the next hour and fifteen minutes they zoomed in on the island, dropping bombs and strafing the American positions.

Soon Carlson learned that the bombing and strafing were just the beginning. The big flying boats had another mission, even more dangerous to the marines. They were bringing in reinforcements. One plane landed off the King's Pier, and thirty-five Japanese soldiers waded ashore. The Kawanishi flying boat was brought under fire by the marines, who disabled it so it could not take off. That meant a loss of another half-dozen reinforcements for the garrison. Carlson moved a .55-caliber antitank gun down to the beach near the

King's Pier, and it began firing on the Japanese aircraft as they came in. The gun shot down one seaplane.

Carlson wondered what had happened to Lieutenant Peatross's boat, until a disheveled and exhausted marine came to the command post to tell the story. Peatross's boat had not gotten the word about the change in orders, and the twelve men had landed at seven A.M. about a mile from the point they had been assigned to take. They had quickly encountered the Japanese and had set fire to an enemy truck, an old Chevrolet. They had gotten into a firefight and killed eight Japanese but had lost three men doing it. The Japanese were now between Peatross's men and the Carlson force. And, Peatross had reported, the Japanese were planning to fly in more reinforcements as soon as possible.

As the afternoon wore away, Carlson pondered. The mission was supposed to last only one day, and that day was nearly over. But the Raiders had not accomplished much. But what *could* they accomplish? Just now they were under heavy sniper fire, and the advance in the government area had been stopped by the reinforcements. Carlson moved his men back a hundred yards, and the Japanese moved up to occupy the positions they had just vacated. Another flight of Japanese bombers came over. They must have been instructed by radio by the previous group, for they bombed where the Americans had been an hour earlier, raining their bombs down on the Japanese troops.

Down south on the island, Lieutenant Peatross was trying to move up to make contact with the Carlson force, but the Japanese had him stopped. He was talking about moving out independently and getting back to the beach and to the submarines, as he had been instructed.

Carlson was also preparing for the withdrawal. He sent men back to the beach to uncover the rubber boats. He was quite sure that the Mille and Jaluit bases would be preparing some unpleasant surprises for him if he stayed in his position. It would soon grow dark, and he did not want to wait for the next day.

Assessing the mission, Carlson had to have a sense of failure, and he did. He had not accomplished anything like the results he had wanted; he had hoped to overrun the island in the morning and spend the day at leisure picking up useful military information from prisoners and papers. Instead, he was engaged in a constant firefight and his men were more or less pinned down. But out there at sea, four miles away, the submarines were waiting for darkness, and then they would come in closer for the rendezvous. It was time for the Raiders to begin to move out.

Hoping against hope, Lieutenant Colonel Carlson continued to hang on a little longer. Six P.M. came and the shadows were growing long. Six-thirty came, and it was growing darker. Reluctantly he gave the order, and it was passed up front and all along the line. The Raiders were to retreat back to the beach, board their boats, and go out to the submarines. They had only an hour until the tide would be right for the withdrawal, and then they had only about two hours in which to make it. Carlson headed for the beach to supervise the movement. It was time to go.

—— 6 ——
Getting Out

It was dark by seven P.M. as the rubber boats were made ready for the returning Raiders. They would have only about an hour and a half of safe time to get through the surf with the tide, and then make rendezvous with the submarines. The *Nautilus* and the *Argonaut* were already moving out of the safety of deep water into the shallows to pick up the men as the battle line moved back toward the ocean beach. As the platoons came back to the command post, led by native policemen, they reported in to Major Roosevelt and Lieutenant Colonel Carlson, and the officers began to count noses. Eleven men had been killed in the day's fighting, and twenty had been wounded. Carlson conferred with Joe Miller, the chief of the native police force, who had been helping the Raiders all day long. Miller promised that the police would find the bodies of the dead marines and give them an honorable burial.

Then it was time to go. The boats were taken to the edge of the surf and the men clambered in and began to paddle through. The wounded went out in the first boats, PFC Le Francois, with five bullets in his shoulder, Lieutenant Charles Lamb, who had been wounded twice, and eighteen others. Lieutenant Colonel Carlson waited on the shore; his boat would be the last to leave. It was part of his responsibility as the leader of the battalion, but he might have left it to Major Roosevelt. Not Evans Carlson. With him remained a squad of men, the rear guard, who made sure that the Japanese did not mount another banzai charge, as the boats were moving and the force was at its most vulnerable.

Now the trouble really began. Carlson had known that the outboard motors' real value was going to be getting the boats out of the surf on the return trip to the submarines. But now they did not have any motors, and the men would have to bring the rounded, awkward boats out by sheer strength. It was one matter to paddle a slim dugout canoe through island surf, but quite another to maneuver a floppy rubber boat. The boats headed into the towering waves. They no sooner recovered from one than another was slapping down on them, filling the craft with water. By the second wave the boats were full of water to the gunwales, and the men were alternately paddling and bailing as fast as they could. The outboard motors were completely useless, just weighting down the boats. So the motors were thrown overboard into the surf as the men tried to get the boats through.

It was nearly impossible, and only seven boats made it through the surf, five to the *Nautilus* and two more to the *Argonaut*. Seventy-three of the two hundred marines were safe, but what of the others?

Their situation grew more desperate by the moment. One boat after another capsized, and the men struggled back through the surf to the island, to arrive exhausted and throw themselves on the sand. Le Francois, the man with the five bullet wounds, had lost a great deal of blood, and when his boat capsized he disappeared in the heavy surf. Lieutenant Lamb also went under, but someone saw him and pulled him back to the island, where he was revived. Several other marines nearly drowned. When they got back to the island, many boats were stove in, and the men had lost nearly all their weapons, ammunition, compasses, radios, and even canteens. After an hour the ordeal was over, and the exhausted Raiders lay on the beach, wondering what was going to happen to them. Most of the wounded had made it to the submarines, but four stretcher cases and several walking wounded were still on the island. Offshore, the submarines waited, and the doctors and corpsmen took care of the wounded. They were scheduled to leave under cover of darkness for Pearl Harbor, but they would not desert the 120 men left ashore.

Lieutenant Colonel Carlson organized his puny defenses ashore. The remaining weapons were rounded up and a defense perimeter was established to prevent the Japanese from walking in on them. The perimeter had just been drawn when a Japanese patrol approached, and was challenged by Marine Jessie Hawkins. A firefight followed, and Hawkins killed three Japanese before they began firing on him from both sides and wounded him. Another marine dragged

Hawkins through the sand to the safety of the beach, and the doctor treated his wound.

All the radios had gone into the sea, so communication had to be established by flashlight and Morse code. The message from the submarines was encouraging: "We will stay with you until you get off. Try to make it before Christmas."

That night the Raiders shivered on the sand and waited. Down the beach Lieutenant Peatross and his men got into a fight with a Japanese patrol, and afterward got back to their submarine in their boat. But the main body was still ashore at daylight. As dawn broke, Lieutenant Colonel Carlson dispatched patrols to try to find food and ammunition. They were looking for Japanese, but the Japanese were not eager for a fight just then. The Raiders saw only three enemy soldiers, and they did not fire on the marines.

Major Roosevelt took the strongest men and four boats and tried to make it through the surf that morning. After a struggle they succeeded. Aboard the submarine Major Roosevelt conferred with the commanders. Five Raiders volunteered to go back ashore to take food and ammunition and weapons to the beleaguered men. They also took tow lines with them so that the other boats could be towed through the surf. They set out—Sergeant Dallas Cook, Sergeant Allard, PFC Richard Olbert, Private John Kerns, and Private Donald Robertson. They had made it about halfway when suddenly Japanese scout seaplanes appeared overhead to attack the submarines, but the skippers took both subs down before the planes could make an attack. The planes then turned their attention to the five marines in the rubber boat. They came down low, strafing, and sank the boat. The five marines began to swim, but the Japanese came back and they strafed the men one by one until all five were dead.

At this point, midmorning of the second day, Lieutenant Colonel Carlson and about seventy men were still holding out on the island. Their situation was desperate, they were short of food and water, and they did not have enough ammunition to hold out against a sustained Japanese attack.

But there was no attack. The Japanese remaining on the island had holed up somewhere, perhaps frightened by the submarines and not knowing how many marines were ashore or their circumstances. The Raider patrols returned to the perimeter to report that they had gone as far as On Chong's wharf and had killed three Japanese soldiers. They did not see any other signs of opposition.

So Lieutenant Colonel Carlson calmly went on with his interrupted mission. He led a patrol to the end of the island to get what intelligence he could about the area. They found the dead marines and turned them over to Police Chief Joe Miller, who promised to bury them. (He did. Months later Carlson returned to Makin and Miller showed him the neat graves of eighteen marines.)

Back at the perimeter, Lieutenant Colonel Carlson dispatched a strong swimmer to go out to the submarines to tell them that the Raiders would make another attempt to get past the surf that night after darkness fell. The fate of that one rescuing rubber boat destroyed by the Japanese air force had convinced him that it was too dangerous to try during daylight. No one knew when another flight of Japanese aircraft might appear.

With most of the day left to him, Lieutenant Colonel Carlson continued to collect intelligence. He took out another patrol. They found several dead Japanese and searched the bodies for intelligence material. They also destroyed all the Japanese installations they could find. They burned down a radio station and smashed the equipment. They blew up several antiaircraft guns. They set fire to a cache of gasoline.

Lieutenant Lamb recovered from his wound enough to take part in the activity. He spotted a sloop anchored offshore on the lagoon side and rowed out with two men to investigate. As they approached they heard a shot, and then a grenade explosion. The boat had been manned by a single guard, and when he saw the marines approaching, he had committed suicide. The wisdom of Carlson's decision to refrain from making any attempt to get through the surf until after darkness fell was confirmed later. Three more flights of Japanese seaplanes came over the island that day and attacked. But they were still operating on the original intelligence from the first planes to arrive, and they attacked all the positions on the old firing line, where the marines had been on the afternoon of the first day. They did not find the marine command post. The miracle of the day was the reappearance of marine Le Francois with his five bullet wounds. He had been thrown out of the boat and washed ashore half dead. But he had survived and managed to find his way to the command post.

Darkness came that evening suddenly, as it does in the tropics. At 7:30 the signalman was again working with his flashlight and was soon in touch with the surfaced submarines. Lieutenant Colonel Carlson did not believe he could get his weakened men and his walking wounded and stretcher cases off the island through the surf. The alternative was to move across to the lagoon side, where there was no surf. But this would mean an extremely dangerous voyage for the submarines, which would have to go into very shallow water. If Japanese planes attacked, the subs would not be able to crash-dive. Further, Carlson's men were in no condition to drag their boats across the island.

But they could paddle to the entrance to the lagoon if they could get through the surf, and that would be a safer place to meet. So Carlson sent a message by flashlight and Morse code to the submarines, suggesting the lagoon rendezvous. There was no answer. The shore repeated the message. Finally the answer came.

"Who?"

Carlson understood. The men of the submarines were afraid of a trap. Were they really in touch with the Raiders, or with some English-speaking Japanese?

But how could Carlson reassure them?

The submarines provided the answer with a new message.

"Who followed my father?"

That was a question that no one but Evans Carlson could answer. On the long voyage from Pearl Harbor, Carlson and Navy Commander Haines had talked about many things. Since Haines's father had been a marine officer, they had much in common. The men had argued about marine matters, one of them being the name of the officer who had followed Haines's father as adjutant of the U.S. Marine Corps. It had been Squeegie Long, said Haines.

Carlson understood the question. This was no time to argue about the answer.

"Squeegie" went back the message from the shore,

and the fears of the submariners were allayed. They would come around the island and brave the shallows to get the Raiders off.

During the explorations of the day, Carlson's men had found an outrigger canoe on the shore. Now they had that canoe and four sound rubber boats to take seventy men out to sea safely.

The day had been hot and dry, the sea almost calm. So the outboard motors of two of the boats were finally started by an optimist. Surprisingly, they ran. The boats were lashed together, and the stretcher cases loaded aboard first. Then came the walking wounded. It was nearly nine P.M. before they could get going, but the able-bodied men paddled, and the motors helped the boats along, and they reached Flink Point, the place of rendezvous, at about 11:30. There were no unpleasant surprises, no lights showed on the shore, and by midnight all the men in the boats were aboard the submarines.

Once again Lieutenant Colonel Carlson counted noses. And this time he had a shock. A dozen men were missing. Carlson had thought these men were with Lieutenant Peatross and Peatross had thought they were with Carlson. In the confusion of the failed attempts to reach the submarines, they had been forgotten. And they were still ashore. It was too late to go back. The submarines had to get moving and get out of shallow water and be prepared to dive at dawn. No one knew where the twelve men were, and there was no time to search for them. So the submarines started off, abandoning a dozen marines to fate.

* * *

On the way back to Pearl Harbor the two doctors and the corpsmen aboard the submarines treated the wounded. The exhausted Raiders slept their way home, and Colonel Carlson spent his hours in the wardroom, considering the results of his raid. He really did not know much about it. They had (by submarine gunfire) sunk a 3,500-ton island trader and a patrol boat. They had burned up the Japanese stocks of gasoline and wrecked their defense installations. They had caused the destruction of two seaplanes. They had killed perhaps fifty or a hundred Japanese, there was no real way of telling. They had lost eighteen men killed, seven drowned in the surf, and fourteen wounded, plus the dozen missing men presumed to be still on the island.

In the end they had done exactly what they set out to do, find out what was going on in the Gilberts, which was not much, if Makin was typical, and they had reason to believe it was.

The submarines arrived back at the base in Pearl Harbor. They were greeted by a brass band, and by Admiral Nimitz, who brought half of his staff down to congratulate them. Their operation had been carried out in secrecy, but now that it was finished, the veil was lifted and the reporters were given access to the Raiders. The navy needed some good publicity, and the American people needed a success story, for just then the battle for Guadalcanal was going very badly.

Besides publicity there were medals. Sergeant Thomason was awarded the Medal of Honor, posthumously, for his leadership of the fighting men who moved up on the battle line against the Japanese on August 17. Lieutenant Colonel Carlson and Major

Roosevelt were both awarded the Navy Cross for their execution of the operation. And there were other medals.

But the best part of the story was not told and could not be. Nimitz and his radio intelligence officers knew that the Carlson raid had been more successful than anybody knew. For when the Japanese high command learned of the attack on the Gilberts, coming as it did shortly after the landings on Guadalcanal, the Japanese did not know quite what to make of it. They had thought originally that the Guadalcanal landings were no more than a raid, too, and had sent only a battalion of troops to face more than a division of marines. That move had been disastrous to one of Japan's crack assault troop battalions. So when the word of the Makin landing came, the Imperial High Command diverted a task force of cruisers, destroyers, and transport ships from the reinforcement of Guadalcanal to the reinforcement of the Gilberts. When they arrived, of course, they found the Raiders long gone, except for the dozen marines abandoned on the island. They captured the nine surviving marines in short order. The prisoners were taken to Kwajalein in the Marshall Islands. Vice Admiral Koiso Abe ordered their execution as spies. Captain Hashio Obara, the commander of the Kwajalein garrison, did not like the decision but there was nothing he could do about it. He called for volunteers to kill the Americans. There were no volunteers. Then Obara ordered four of his officers to execute the marines. They had to obey the direct order. On October 16, the nine marines were beheaded one after the other, by samurai sword. Captain Obara showed his distaste for the task by choosing the date, which was the day on which the Japanese honor their own war dead. (His reluctance to execute the Americans saved his life later when war crimes trials were held in Japan. Captain Obara was sent to prison for ten years for committing an atrocity. Admiral Abe, who insisted on it, was hanged. Of course, none of this was known to the Americans at Pearl Harbor and had not occurred when the Carlson Raiders came back from Makin.) The Carlson raid had diverted the Japanese task force, which relieved the Americans at Guadalcanal from a new threat at a time when they were in desperate battle to hold on. Admiral Nimitz could not say a word about it because his information came from the radio interception of Japanese messages and to admit it would be to tell the Japanese that the Americans had broken the Japanese naval codes. So Lieutenant Colonel Carlson and his Raiders never got the full credit for the success of their mission, which helped to turn the war around in the Solomons at a time when the Japanese seemed to be winning every naval battle and the marines were under siege from sea and air.

—— 7 ——

Guadalcanal

As the Raiders moved ashore at Tulagi across the coral reef, on the other side of Lunga Channel the marines of the 2nd Marine Division landed on Guadalcanal, the site of the brand-new Japanese naval air base at Lunga Point. As with the Tulagi invasion, the landing was almost uneventful. The marines stormed ashore and headed for the Japanese encampment on the shore. They found the Japanese gone, although food was still in the cooking tents and on the tables.

They discovered a large amount of construction material, including bulldozers and a hundred trucks. There were some weapons, mostly small arms, and ammunition. They had completely surprised the troops of the Japanese Pioneer units (construction battalions) who had been sent to Guadalcanal and were just finishing up the construction of the air field. The Japanese who were not unlucky enough to get in the way of the marines fled into the jungle and headed south, away from the airfield area. Within a matter of hours the marines had established camp and were apparently in undisputed control.

From the Tulagi radio station the word was flashed to Japanese headquarters at Rabaul and Truk that a force of Americans had landed and was overrunning the island. The Tulagi garrison apologized to the emperor for failing to prevent the landings. Then the radio went dead, victim of an eight-inch shell from the cruiser *San Juan,* and no more was heard at Truk and Rabaul from the southern Solomons.

The American marines were soon busily loading off supplies and rebuilding the road up to the airfield, which they promptly christened Henderson Field, in honor of a marine officer who had been killed in the battle for Midway two months earlier. Marine General Alexander Vandegrift was not fooled, however. He knew that it was all too easy and would not remain that way. The Americans had captured Guadalcanal, but could they hold it? The Japanese would fight, there was no question about that, but how and when?

At Rabaul the Japanese Imperial Navy's 10th Air Fleet was ordered to find out what was going on, so air units were sent to attack the Americans and return with some intelligence. They came within a matter of hours, they bombed the ships and the beaches, and they returned to Rabaul to report that there had indeed been a landing, the seaplane base at Tulagi was destroyed, and Americans were ashore on Guadalcanal. But they did not give any indication of the strength of the American force.

*   *   *

In Japan at the Kagoshima anchorage of the Combined Fleet, Admiral Yamamoto was inclined to believe that the American landings on Tulagi and Guadalcanal had been of a piece with the Battle of the Coral Sea, fought in May, when the Americans had destroyed the seaplane base just after it was established, but had not tried to capture and hold Tulagi or Guadalcanal. Yamamoto had a good idea of the strengths and weaknesses of the Pacific Fleet, and he estimated that following the Pearl Harbor raid he would have about a year before the going began to get tough. Just eight months had passed, and he found it difficult to believe—along with General MacArthur, Admiral Ghormley, and Admiral Fletcher—that the Americans were yet capable of launching and sustaining an offensive.

Yamamoto was extremely interested in the intelligence that the Japanese pilots had seen American carriers off Guadalcanal. His major interest was the destruction of the American fleet, so he dispatched Vice Admiral Chuichi Nagumo and elements of the battle fleet to the south to engage and destroy the Americans. As for the American troops ashore, once the U.S. fleet was defeated, it would be a simple enough matter to dispose of them, if indeed they did not leave the island. It should be a task for a battalion.

At Rabaul on New Britain Island, several hundred miles north of Guadalcanal, General Haruyoshi Hyukatake was not at all concerned about the reports of the American landing, except as a curiosity. Under the Japanese division of military responsibility in this war, the navy had to take care of the forward island bases, to defend and supply them. Hyukatake's enormous army command at Rabaul was being developed for the invasion of Australia. Hundreds of thousands of tons of ammunition, food, and supply were being stockpiled at Rabaul for future use. Imperial General Headquarters in Tokyo was planning a whole series of assaults to renew the drive on Australian-held New Guinea, then to take the islands around the northern side of Australia, and finally to invade Australia itself. That was why General Hyukatake was there, to prepare and later carry out army operations. The army was not concerned with the handful of small islands north of Australia that were really just part of the navy base system.

Therefore, when the Japanese attack on the Americans at Guadalcanal began, in those first few hours after the marine invasion, it came from the air and then from the sea. Admiral Yamamoto's planes came down from Rabaul, and his destroyers from Rabaul and Truk, to shell the airfield on Guadalcanal and prevent the Americans from using it. His carriers began the search for Admiral Frank Jack Fletcher's carrier task force, but they did not find it. Admiral Fletcher did not want to fight, and he was moving around far in the south, avoiding an engagement.

But as far as land operations were concerned, the marines had virtually no opposition in those first few days after the landings. The real problem for General Vandegrift was supply. After the landing, the supply of the beachhead had been stopped because of the bombings of the transports and cargo ships, and Admiral Turner's landing task force had moved out to sea for safety. The failure of Admiral Fletcher to protect the supply train made it impossible for Turner, and he stayed away from the beaches. Thus General Vandegrift, with more than ten thousand men ashore at this time, was immediately faced with a critical shortage of food, weapons, ammunition, and gasoline.

It was about two weeks before the Japanese at Rabaul learned what was really happening at Guadalcanal and demanded that Admiral Yamamoto do something to stop it. One cause of the complacency, as noted, was the raid by Lieutenant Colonel Carlson's 2nd Raider Battalion on Makin just ten days after the marines landed on Tulagi and Guadalcanal. The Japanese naval authorities were inclined to believe that the Guadalcanal operation was a twin to the Makin. The Americans would remain for a while, then retreat, and air operations out of Guadalcanal could be resumed.

But the pilots from Rabaul began coming back with reports of many air battles, and of much activity on the ground. They indicated that there were several thousand troops in occupation. Occasionally Admiral Turner would try to run some ships in to supply Vandegrift, and when the Japanese pilots saw them, they reported that the force ashore had to be a large one. Soon General Hyukatake's intelligence officers knew that the American troops ashore were called "marines," but at that moment they did not know what marines were. They queried some of the naval officers in the area and discovered that the marines were the U.S. Navy's shock troops. And then General Hyukatake began to sit up and take notice.

But back in Japan the feeling of complacency was hard to shake. Imperial General Headquarters was not much concerned. For so long had the Japanese forces been rolling up victories, it seemed impossible the pattern could change. Since the surrender of Singapore by the British to a Japanese army about half the size of the British, Imperial General Headquarters had been putting out propaganda saying that the Americans and British were effete Westerners with no taste for fighting and very little ability to sustain a war. They had come to believe this themselves and it affected their whole outlook.

What was happening at sea around Guadalcanal did nothing to disabuse the Japanese or decrease their arrogance. The Japanese had control of the air, and of the sea. Their bombers and fighters came down from Rabaul every day to strike at Guadalcanal, and the Americans and Australians had to pull out all the stops to get any planes into the air to oppose them. The "Cactus Air Force," as the Guadalcanal contingent was called, was fighting hard just to stay alive. Gasoline for the planes was in very short supply, and because of the inability of Admiral Turner to supply the island by cargo ship, gasoline was brought in by submarine.

As for the sea, the Japanese were winning one naval battle after another. The most disastrous of all was fought late in August just off Savo Island. The allies lost four cruisers and had many other ships badly damaged, while the Japanese did not lose a ship. Admiral Matome Ugaki, chief of staff to Admiral Yamamoto, noted that the Americans were losing one ship after another but continued to bring in more vessels. He was surprised at their staying power but confident of the future. Every night Japanese warships came down "through the slot," as the narrow channel off Savo was called, to bombard Henderson Field and the marine camps. So it seemed that victory for the Japanese was just around the corner and that all that was necessary was to send in a small land force to wipe out the offending Americans on Guadalcanal.

Yamamoto chose a reinforced battalion of shock troops to do the job. The unit was one of the best of Japan's naval landing troop units, the equivalent of the U.S. Marines. It was commanded by Colonel Kiyonao Ichiki. It was available at this point because the Ichiki force had been originally slated to land at Midway and destroy the American ground forces there, but the landings had never come off. The disaster of the sea battle of Midway, at which the Japanese had lost four aircraft carriers, had put an end to the Midway invasion before it was scarcely begun. So, once the need for ground forces on Guadalcanal was established, Colonel Ichiki was dispatched with a thousand men and minimal supply. The Ichiki force was landed by destroyer transports on the southern end of the island and ordered to break through and capture the airfield. Nobody in authority expected it to take long. Early in September Colonel Ichiki's men were moving through the jungle from Taivu, east of Lunga Point, headed for the airfield.

From aerial observers General Vandegrift had word of the coming of the Japanese. He did not know how large the attacking force was, and he decided he needed troop reinforcement on Guadalcanal. The logical place to find it was Tulagi, for there Lieutenant Colonel Edson's 1st Raider Battalion and its supporting units had just about wiped out all the Japanese stragglers, and there was little for them to do. So General Vandegrift put in a call for "Red Mike," as Colonel Edson was known. He would bring over the 1st Raider Battalion and the 1st Parachute Battalion and they would establish a defense of Henderson Field against the Japanese.

On September 7 the Raiders and the parachute troops boarded the destroyer transports *Manley* and *McKean* and two smaller vessels and were shipped across the sound to Guadalcanal. They set up their camp west of the Lunga River near Kukum. Once the camp was established, the Raiders sat down to wait. But not for long. Coastwatchers reported that there were Japanese troops on Savo, at the western end of Guadalcanal. A Japanese submarine had been seen lying off the shore there, and fires had been observed. They constituted a threat to the marines because the ground troops could signal the submarines and make it even harder for Admiral Turner to bring supplies in to Guadalcanal. So General Vandegrift ordered Colonel Edson to take care of the Japanese on Savo Island.

On September 12 the destroyer transports *Little* and *Gregory* embarked two companies of the 1st Raider Battalion. The distance was not far, and before dark they were waiting offshore. They waited all night while Colonel Edson made the plans. Lieutenant Colonel Griffith would again lead the troops ashore, while Red Mike stayed aboard and coordinated their efforts. The marines would land at the northern end of the island and divide into two forces, then search both sides of the island. But the next morning, after the ships had moved cautiously into the shore at Savo Island, they landed and met a group of Solomon Islanders who informed them that contrary to reports there were no Japanese left on the island. Those fires and the submarine must have represented the escape of some of the troops from Tulagi, who could have swum or gone by canoe to Savo and been picked up by a submarine.

The Raiders did not take the word of the islanders, but they turned out to be quite right; there were no Japanese. So after a wasted day the Raiders went back to the ships and were transported back to Guadalcanal. But not to rest. They were supposed to remain aboard the destroyers that night, but the word was slow in getting to them so they went ashore. That night the "Tokyo Express" had come down the slot again, three destroyers, bringing transports and more troops. The destroyers *Little* and *Gregory* were patrolling off Lunga Point. They were sighted by the Japanese and attacked. The old four-stack American destroyers were of WWI vintage, which was why they were used primarily for troop transport. They were no match for the modern Japanese ships. The two destroyers were destroyed. More iron for the bottom of the bay.

But the next morning the attack on Taivu Point was still scheduled. Intelligence, derived mostly from native villagers in the Taivu area, indicated that the Japanese down there were starving and very weak. Two more destroyers, the *Manley* and the *McKean* again were readied, with Red Mike Edson leading the troops aboard. A pair of tuna boats from California had also been enlisted for this task, and the remaining Raiders were taken on. They headed for battle.

The day was gray and rainy. The tropical rain came down very hard, and the wind was cold. At dawn the marines were on deck, ready to get into the landing craft, and at 5:20 planes from the Cactus Air Force bombed and strafed the area around Tasimboko, where the raiders would land. After the raid they did land, but they found no Japanese where Red Mike Edson had estimated there would be about three thousand enemy troops. They found field pieces and ammunition set up in defense but no troops. The reason was probably that as the Raiders landed, around Taivu Point, heading for Lunga Point, came a pair of American cargo ships that were bringing supplies for the marines, and they were guarded by several destroyers. To the Japanese it appeared that another landing in force was being staged, and they disappeared into the jungle, leaving weapons and supplies behind.

The Raiders began to move out, searching for the Japanese. They saw plenty of evidence of well-trained, well-fed troops, but still no troops. Finally, down near the beach where the last elements from Rabaul had been landed the night before, they did find some Japanese, and a firefight began. Both sides used mortars and the Japanese had artillery pieces. A small stream ran parallel to the shore there. The American left flank was along that stream. The Japanese were on the other side. The Americans moved up to the village, seeing more evidence of Japanese supply. The Japanese outflanked them and moved into the jungle. The marines kept going. They captured several 75mm field pieces. But the Japanese had others, and they were shelling the Raiders and causing many casualties. A single 75mm shell wiped out one whole squad of men. Lieutenant Colonel Edson stopped to take stock. Everything he had seen belied the intelligence that had come from the native Solomon Islanders. These were not half-starved troops but fresh troops with very good equipment and plenty of food. What had happened, of course, was that the natives had been reporting on the remnants of the Pioneers, those survivors of the original marine attack a month before, who had fled into the jungle leaving their food and everything else behind. Those troops had been starving, but they were not the Ichiki detachment of naval landing forces that had just arrived to take the island away from the marines. Edson needed some help.

That day he got it. The two destroyers had landed the marines and then gone back to the Kukum camp. There they picked up the 1st Parachute Battalion and brought them down to join the fighting. The parachute troops were landed just before noon east of the town of Tasimboko. The destroyers were then called on for fire support and began to shell the town. Now the Japanese were outflanked, but they were still much more powerful than Edson had been led to believe. He radioed General Vandegrift's command post for additional help, but Vandegrift had no one to send to him, so he advised Edson to withdraw and come back to Kukum. But Edson could not withdraw. His troops were scattered, with Japanese between the companies and the platoons. At noon Edson was out of contact with A Company.

So the Raiders fought. Shortly after noon they captured the town of Tasimboko, and there they found more field guns, machine guns, and about a half a million rounds of ammunition. Edson now set about getting reorganized. Intelligence officers began checking the Japanese bodies to discover what unit they were facing. They found that these troops had been recently in the Dutch East Indies, but the name Ichiki detachment did not mean anything to them. They blew up the field guns and destroyed the ammunition, and then as soon as all the units were in contact with the command post, Colonel Edson ordered them to go down to the beach to reembark in the ships, as ordered by General Vandegrift. At three o'clock that afternoon the men were moving down toward the landing craft, and not a moment too soon, because Colonel Ichiki had decided that this was not a major landing after all, and was bringing his forces together to wipe out the enemy at Tasimboko. The Raiders kept a rear guard on the beach until 5:30 that afternoon, and there was some sporadic firing, but the Japanese were still not organized for battle then, and so the last men got into the boats, the destroyers covered them, and the debarkation was soon complete. That night they moved back to Kukum, and the Japanese recovered what they could of their supplies and prepared to resume their assault on Henderson Field, delayed by the activities of the day. In fact, the loss of the field guns and ammunition and many other supplies was fatal to the Japanese effort. There had been too few men sent in the first place, and too few supplies. Now Colonel Ichiki realized that his situation was desperate. But he had been given his orders, and he had no recourse but to carry them out. He began to move.

That night the American destroyers carrying the Raiders headed for Lunga Channel. The Japanese bombers came over at dusk and bombed Tulagi. The destroyers zigzagged and avoided any trouble. The ships pulled into shore off Kukum and the Raiders went ashore. That night Lieutenant Colonel Edson reported that he had run into tough opposition from well-trained and well-armed troops. General Vandegrift's intelligence officers were able to make much more of the papers that Edson delivered than his people had. They soon knew that they were facing some six thousand Japanese, maybe more. For General Hyukatake was reinforcing the Ichiki detachment. General Vandegrift also learned that he could expect an attack very soon to drive the Americans away from Henderson Field.

— 8 —

The Thin and Dirty Line

General Vandegrift knew that the Japanese were going to be on him very soon. The disastrous results of the Battle of Savo Island, in which the Allies lost three American cruisers and one Australian cruiser, was proof positive that the Japanese controlled the seas. And Vice Admiral Frank Jack Fletcher had long before yielded to them control of the air by refusing to put his two aircraft carriers in jeopardy by operating them around Guadalcanal. The marines were short of supply. Admiral Yamamoto recognized the urgency of the situation, and had almost from the beginning when he sent from Japan a message to Rear Admiral Gunichi Mikawa, telling him to support the Japanese army forces that were moving into Guadalcanal to try to wrest control from the Americans.

General Kiyotake Kawaguchi's military force on Guadalcanal was being augmented almost nightly by reinforcements from Rabaul brought in on the "Tokyo Express" of destroyers that came down the slot. Kawaguchi's mission was to capture Henderson Field, an enterprise in which he was to be supported by the navy. At Rabaul, General Hyukatake suggested that they ought to send an entire division to Guadalcanal, but General Kawaguchi had said he really did not need it, the troops he had could defeat the Americans handily. The plan called for a four-pronged attack on September 12. Japanese troops already ashore would hit the marines on both flanks and from the rear, while from the sea would come a new amphibious assault. That ought to take care of the American threat once and for all. By October 10, said General Kawaguchi, he would have control of Guadalcanal and the navy could resume its plans for attack on Australia by air, and General Hyukatake could move his headquarters down from Rabaul to Guadalcanal preparatory to the army's assault on Australia.

General Vandegrift had made the same mistake that General Hyukatake had made earlier: he had seriously underestimated his enemy. When the Raiders had gone to Tasimboko, Vandegrift had suggested that there were only about five hundred Japanese on the island. The Solomon Islanders had assured him that there were many many Japanese, but with their limited arithmetic, they did not get the message through to the Americans that the number could be counted in the thousands. So Lieutenant Colonel Red Mike Edson had gone to assault Tasimboko and had there learned some of the unpleasant facts of life. Most important was the document the marines captured which unveiled General Kawaguchi's plan of attack on Henderson Field. Three battalions of Japanese were to attack from the south. One battalion would strike west across the Tenaru River. Two more battalions would cross the Lunga River and attack from the northwest. Then would come the seaborne assault on the beaches.

Even with this information in hand, General Vandegrift felt that his force could handle the threat. He sent a battalion from the 1st Marine Regiment to reinforce the Tenaru River positions. On the western side, Lieutenant Colonel F. C. Biebush's 3rd Battalion was well entrenched on a small grassy ridge south of Kukum. Biebush had several 75mm pack howitzers too. The airstrip lay inland from Kukum, to the east of the Lunga River, and behind it General Vandegrift had built his command post. Headquarters was protected by the 1st Amphibian Tractor Battalion on the west, the Pioneer Battalion up against the Lunga River near its headwaters, and the Engineers just west of Vandegrift's command post. Between the command post and Henderson Field were several batteries of 105mm howitzers under the command of Colonel E. H. Price.

Altogether, the disposition seemed to be just about as satisfactory as Vandegrift could expect.

When Lieutenant Colonel Edson came back from the Tasimboko raid, however, he took a look at the dispositions and the terrain and offered another opinion. South of Vandegrift's command post was a hog-backed ridge that ran parallel to the Lunga River. On three sides it was surrounded by jungle, but on the fourth side, the north, it was a gentle grassy slope that led down to Vandegrift headquarters, to the artillery, and to Henderson Field.

When General Vandegrift heard Lieutenant Colonel Edson's suggestion that the Japanese would mass an attack up through the jungle against that ridge, he was skeptical. Then Edson told him what he had seen at Tasimboko: the Japanese hacking trails through the deep jungle, which was how they had escaped the trap laid by the Raiders, even though they had lost much ammunition and supply.

So General Vandegrift told Lieutenant Colonel Edson that he should bring up his Raiders and parachute troops and defend that ridgeline against attack.

Red Mike Edson went back down to Kukum that day and told his boys that they would be moving out to the ridge just above the general's new headquarters. Someone asked why.

"We're going back to a rest area," said Red Mike.

Lieutenant Colonel Harry Torgerson took the parachute troops to the eastern flank of the ridge. The Raiders moved up in the center and right, with platoons strung out on the right flank, or western side, facing the Lunga River. They began to dig in. The digging was hard going—it meant fighting coral rock with a two-foot entrenching tool, and some of the men were not careful about the depth of their foxholes. But they learned. Next morning, September 11, a flight of Japanese bombers and fighters came over Henderson Field, as they did every day, and this time they bombed the ridge rest area. Marines were killed and wounded that day, and the rest then began really to dig in. They dug and dug and dug. And when they were finished, they had quite respectable positions to defend. That night the Tokyo Express thundered down on Guadalcanal as usual, the Japanese destroyers delivering more troops to General Kawaguchi for the next day's attack. They bombarded Henderson Field as usual, and some of the shells fell on this ridge. But there were no casualties. It would take a direct hit by a shell to reach the dug-in marines.

On the morning of September 12, the marines were at work again. They unrolled barbed wire and strung it along the bottom of the ridge, facing the jungle. They brought up extra ammunition for the machine guns, the Browning automatic rifles, and the Garand rifles and carbines, and boxes of hand grenades.

Down the ridge toward Henderson Field, the artillerymen adjusted their sights and prepared to fire into the jungle as close to the ridge line as possible.

The marines were preparing for action. So were the Japanese. They sent a number of patrols to test the defenses of the ridge line that day. The main Japanese force was brought up the jungle trails to a point northeast of the ridge to bivouac during the daylight hours. The Japanese attackers were separated into four units. Three groups would attack the ridge frontally, and the fourth would move down to outflank the marines along the Tenaru River and link up with the seaborne assault troops. The Japanese came to bomb again on September 12. But once more the deep foxholes on the ridge line protected the marines. There were few casualties.

When darkness fell, the Japanese probing of the marine lines became more insistent. Soon it was pitch-dark. Then it began to rain.

All was fairly quiet until nine P.M. The Japanese were waiting for something. The sounds of the jungle were muted by the rain, and the marines strained their ears for clues to Japanese intentions.

At nine P.M. a Japanese plane came over and dropped a flare. The marines tensed, expecting the infantry attack to begin. But the flare was a signal to the Tokyo Express, which was once more bearing down on Guadalcanal, and in less than half an hour the Express arrived: a cruiser and three destroyers, to land more troops and to bombard Henderson Field and the area all around it. Perhaps this night the gunners aboard the ships were cognizant of the coming attack on land. They did not bombard the ridge. Their shells were short, not even landing on Henderson Field but in the jungles to the west of it, where they did no harm since there were no American troops closer than the Biebush line on the coast.

But less than an hour after the Tokyo Express had gone back up the slot, a rocket exploded in the air above the jungle. It was the signal for the Japanese infantry attack. Most of the Japanese started up the ridge, while some went along it and probed until they found a way up through the marine positions. They shouted and screamed and sang as they came.

"Tenno heika banzai," they cried. "May His Majesty the Emperor live ten thousand years."

"Shinde, marin," they shouted. "Die, Marine."

"Marin no chi o notte. . . ." "Taste marine blood."

And on they came, shooting and shouting and hurling grenades. Some Japanese got in through the line of foxholes, and some marines died. So did some Japanese. The marine platoon on the right flank of the line was cut off by a squad of Japanese who staged a bayonet attack, and others moved around to try to encircle the flank. But the cutoff marine platoon came out of the foxholes and fought their way back to the main line of defense. On the other flank the parachutists were enveloped, but they rallied and drove the Japanese out of the pocket. The marine artillery down in the valley began firing close to the jungle side of the ridge, and the accurate barrage disrupted the Japanese attack. The Raiders added the fire from their own mortars. And the Japanese retreated into the jungle. Before dawn, on September 13, all was quiet along the ridge line.

As the sun rose on the morning of September 13, the marine line was holding, but the Raiders were very tired. They had gotten no sleep the night before. General Vandegrift was worried because he had only a tiny reserve under Colonel Whaling, south of the airfield. Lieutenant Colonel Edson was concerned because he did not have enough men to make a counterattack. He reported to General Vandegrift, dirty and bedraggled as he was. His blouse was torn by two bullets which had come through, only grazing him. Major Kenneth Bailey had a ragged hole through his helmet which showed where a Japanese bullet had grazed his head. There were at least two thousand Japanese in the jungle behind the ridge, Edson said. The marines must have killed or wounded six or seven hundred of them, and the back of the attack was at least badly bent. But the Raiders had taken casualties too. One squad had been holding an exposed position at the top of the ridge on the south side. The Japanese had made one attack after another on this squad, trying to get through the line. Finally there were only four men alive, less than half the squad, and they were in deadly peril. PFC Ray Herndon had been hit in the belly and he was dying. He told the other three men to retreat; he would hold the line, and he asked for the .45 automatic pistol one of them had, just in case he ran out of rifle ammunition. They left him there.

Lieutenant Colonel Lewis E. Johnson was wounded by a grenade in the fighting. And the fighting did not end with night, Colonel Edson reported. Next morning the casualties, including Colonel Johnson, were being taken down to the aid camp near Kukum for treatment. The road to Kukum led down the ridge, which was in the open, and so the Japanese fired on the truck that was taking them down. A machine gun opened up on the road. The truck driver was wounded, and the truck screeched to a stop. The Japanese increased their fire. Lieutenant Colonel Johnson got out of the back and up to the cab and got in. He tried to start the truck. It would not start. He put the truck in gear and used the starter to propel it, bucking and stopping, out of range of the Japanese machine gun. There he was able to start the flooded engine and he drove to the field hospital, where the wounded men were taken out, including the truck driver. Then Colonel Johnson drove back up the ridge to pick up another load of wounded.

Colonel Edson predicted the Japanese would be back the next night. That day the marines improved their foxholes, and Red Mike toured the perimeter and gave them advice on how to do it better. Some of the marines were busy as snipers, pot-shotting at Japanese in the trees. A number of the enemy had been trapped behind the marine lines when dawn had come, and they had taken to the trees to become snipers. Rifles, machine guns, and BARs were used to flush them out.

The Japanese were tired, too, after having fought their way through the jungle and then spent the night in attacks. But they were confident of victory, particularly when they saw that their planes had control of the sky. What they did not have was artillery; the artillery had been lost at Tasimboko when the Raiders staged their surprise attack on the camp.

As darkness fell, the Japanese prepared for another bayonet attack on the marine lines. A red rocket went up, and they started forward. Most of the line held, but the Japanese found a hole west of the ridge and forced through.

They outflanked one company, but the marines moved back, turned, and made a new defense. At nine P.M. the American artillery went into action, firing at the source of rockets that the Japanese sent up. The guns fired all night long.

At 10:30 the Japanese used a new stratagem. They laid down a smoke screen along the ridge and came charging up, shouting, "Gas attack, gas attack," hoping to persuade the marines to panic. The marines did not panic, but the Japanese attack, conducted by at least two thousand men, was the most furious yet, and it forced the marines back. Colonel Edson brought up his reserves, a company of sixty men under Captain John Sweeney, and they went forward, but then were stuck out in the middle of the Japanese attack, and Edson withdrew them. By this time the marines had been pushed back to the last spur of the ridge, only 1,500 yards from Henderson Field. The Japanese now sent men to infiltrate, and a Japanese officer and two men got as far as the Vandegrift command post, to be killed by the staff. The scene of the action was only a quarter of a mile from the command post. The Japanese would send up a red rocket, a unit would make a banzai charge, come up the slope of the ridge into the teeth of automatic weapons fire, ringed by the artillery fire and the American mortars, and the attack would fail. It happened over and over.

In the light of a Japanese magnesium flare, PFC James Corzine saw a Japanese squad setting up a machine gun. He rushed them with bayonet, stabbed the gunner, and swung the gun around on the Japanese. The other men of the squad fired and killed him, but he had routed them and they did not get the gun back.

Captain Sweeney's company lost all unity, and the men fought as individuals. The paratroopers took a tremendous beating on the left flank. The Tokyo Express came down that night and shelled the field and the ridge. Seven destroyers were involved that night.

The marines took it all and held. By 2:30 the fighting had slackened and Lieutenant Colonel Edson could report that fact to General Vandegrift, plus the prediction that the worst was over for the night and that they would continue to hold.

The fighting continued all night, but it was sporadic and involved small units of men. The big attack had been blunted for the day. As September 14 dawned, the marines began to pull themselves together again. That day the units reported to General Vandegrift. The paratroopers had lost 212 men, more than half their force. The Raiders were cut from 750 able-bodied men to 526. But the slope of the ridge was so littered with the bodies of the dead Japanese that it acquired a new name that day. "Bloody Ridge" was how it would go down in marine history.

As the light firmed up, General Vandegrift called to Henderson Field for air support, and every plane that could fly took off that morning to bomb and strafe the Japanese on the far side of Bloody Ridge and in the jungle. Two other attacks had been made that night, one on Colonel McKelvy's Tenaru River defenses, and one on Colonel Biebush's 3rd Battalion on the west. Neither succeeded.

As daylight broadened on September 14, the Japanese moved back into the deep jungle. General Kawaguchi then took count. He had lost nearly 1,150 men in the past two days. His force had been so cut up that it was no longer possible to launch a major attack and would not be until reinforcements were received. And reinforcements were coming. General Hyukatake now saw that he had been right in the beginning. At least a division of troops was going to be needed to fight the Americans and drive them off Guadalcanal. The marines were going to be reinforced, too, just as soon as troops could be brought in. But there was no rest for the 1st Marine Raider Battalion. They were needed desperately to keep the lines up, and so they stayed, after that vicious battle in which forty of them died and 103 were wounded in one night.

—— 9 ——

The Coming of Pistol Pete

Reinforcements began showing up on Guadalcanal in the middle of September, but the Raiders stayed on. General Vandergrift still needed that 1st Raider Battalion. The first reinforcements were the men of the 7th Marine Regiment, who sailed from Espiritu Santo on September 14 in six transports. Their arrival was delayed because the covering carrier task force stopped to fight (and lose a naval battle; the carrier *Wasp* was sunk and the battleship *North Carolina* was torpedoed but survived; the destroyer *O'Brien* was also torpedoed, seemed to survive, but broke up and sank on the voyage home to America).

The transports milled around at sea for two days, and then Admiral Turner decided to send them on to Guadalcanal without their escort. They arrived at Lunga Roads on September 18 and the defenders of

Guadalcanal had four thousand reinforcements with tanks, trucks, ammunition, and food.

The Japanese continued to make an enormous effort in the air to control the skies over Guadalcanal, but the odds were changing. The bombers came down, but many did not get back. By late September the Japanese had lost more than two hundred planes over Guadalcanal, and the Americans had lost only thirty-two planes. The Japanese still had more planes, but the distance was great from Rabaul, and the attack steadily became more difficult.

The Japanese continued to send the Tokyo Express down the slot at will, bombarding Henderson Field and other installations. They introduced a new tactic: the use of spotter planes at night. Every night two float planes from Rekata Bay's seaplane base appeared over Guadalcanal to drop flares to guide the bombarding of destroyers and cruisers. The marines, always colorful in characterization, came to know these two aircraft as "Washing Machine Charlie" (because of the sound of the plane's engine) and "Louie the Louse." The two planes also dropped antipersonnel bombs in the bivouac areas, just to keep the marines awake and insecure.

By September 18, when the 7th Marines arrived to augment General Vandegrift's defenses, the Japanese had also brought in many reinforcements. They were landed west of the Matanikau River, around Point Cruz. The buildup continued, and General Vandegrift decided he had the strength now to undertake an offensive against the Japanese, to prevent them from launching a new attack. On September 20 Vandegrift pulled Lieutenant Colonel Edson out of the 1st Raider Battalion, promoted him to colonel, gave him command of the 5th Marine Regiment, and told him to undertake an offensive against the Japanese in the Matanikau region.

Lieutenant Colonel Sam Griffith took over the 1st Raider Battalion that day. Colonel Edson informed him that he was going to be back in action very soon.

General Vandegrift wanted to drive the Japanese beyond the Poha River, in order to get them out of artillery range from Henderson Field. But as he considered that course, down from the coastwatchers in the central Solomons came word that the Japanese were building up shipping and aircraft in the Shortlands area, which meant that they must be preparing for a new offensive at Guadalcanal. Therefore, the objective for the moment was confined by General Vandegrift to an attempt to secure the east bank of the Matanikau River. To do this, Lieutenant Colonel Lewis (Chesty) Puller was to take his 1st Battalion of the 7th Marines overland up Grassy Ridge and Mount Austen, six miles southwest of Henderson Field, and cross the Matanikau. Lieutenant Colonel Griffith was to lead the 1st Raider Battalion along the coast, to the mouth of the Matanikau, go up the river, and cross at a place built up by the Japanese called Nippon Bridge. But Lieutenant Colonel Puller's men were new to Guadalcanal, and they soon learned that the terrain was very difficult to cross. The thick jungle impeded their progress, they had to cut their way through with machetes, and as they approached the Mount Austen area, the Japanese, who were there in force, began to attack them. The American advance to the Matanikau slowed perceptibly. Three days after the 7th Marines set out, Colonel Puller could see that they were not going to cross the Matanikau on the date specified, so he turned north to go parallel to the river. He reached the mouth of the river that night and joined the force of Lieutenant Colonel McDougal's 2nd Battalion of Edson's 5th Marines, which had been set up at the mouth as a rear guard to prevent the Japanese from crossing and flanking the marines. Meanwhile, Lieutenant Colonel Griffith headed that day toward Nippon Bridge to do what the 7th Marines had failed to do.

Griffith ran into trouble in the Mount Austen area. The Japanese caught the marines in a clearing and opened a deadly crossfire. Several marines were down immediately, including Major Kenneth Bailey, one of the heroes of Bloody Ridge, who was killed there. To rout the enemy, the Raiders would have to climb a steep hill that commanded the Japanese positions, so they started up. It took four hours to reach the top. When they got there they were greeted by a hail of Japanese fire from well-prepared positions, and Lieutenant Colonel Griffith was badly wounded. When the word of the series of disasters reached Colonel Edson, he recalled the Raiders to the mouth of the Matanikau. They marched back, carrying their dead and wounded, and reached the mouth of the river on September 27.

That day another series of errors caused more confusion. Lieutenant Colonel Puller believed that the 1st Raider Battalion had crossed the Matanikau at Nippon Bridge and then had moved to its objective. That was what they were supposed to have done, to end up south of Point Cruz. A radio transmission that was quite garbled seemed to indicate that they had succeeded. So Lieutenant Colonel Puller sent Major Otho L. Rogers with three companies of his battalion by landing craft up to Point Cruz. The marines landed west of the point and moved inland, to find the 1st

Raiders. Instead, before they had gone inland a quarter of a mile they met a strong party of Japanese who had circled around and attacked from the rear or beach side. Major Rogers was killed. The marines were in a position not unlike that of General Custer at the Little Bighorn. They crowded up on a kunai grass knoll and deployed in a circle to fight off the Japanese all around them. They had lost their radio. The situation looked very bleak. Someone had the idea of taking off their undershirts and improvising a message that might be spotted from the air. It read,

HELP

Later that day an Allied plane pilot spotted the message and reported by radio. Henderson Field got in touch with division headquarters, but just then the area was undergoing the usual Japanese bombing attack, and a bomb had knocked out General Vandegrift's communications system.

Waiting at Kukum, Colonel Puller had the feeling that something was wrong. He got aboard the destroyer *Monssen* and steamed over to Point Cruz. From the hill south of the point, the beleaguered men of the 7th Marines could see the destroyer standing offshore. One sergeant who know Morse code stood out in full view of the Japanese and signaled with his arms to inform the navy what had happened. Colonel Puller then ordered the marines to leave the knoll and move down to the coast. They would be covered by a naval barrage from the *Monssen,* he said. So the two companies fought their way down to the beach while the destroyer sent five-inch shells all around them to keep the Japanese away. They reached the beach and formed a defense perimeter. A shore party came in from the *Monssen* on landing craft with two small boat guns. They covered the 7th Marines while they boarded five landing craft to get out to sea. When the first load of marines went out, the Japanese took the opportunity to bring up more troops, and when the boats came back in, they were hit by very heavy fire. The *Monssen* called for air support, and Henderson Field sent down a dive bomber to work over the area with bombs and strafing, and cover the retreat.

So the men of the 7th Marines escaped the trap, or most of them did. But the cost of this whole failed Matanikau operation had been quite high: sixty marines killed and a hundred wounded, and few Japanese casualties. It had been an ill-conceived operation, based on faulty intelligence about the strength and disposition of the Japanese.

General Vandegrift had made his decision just as General Hyukatake was moving to correct his own past error of sending too few troops to do too much, and was pouring reinforcements into Guadalcanal. He intended to put twenty-five thousand men ashore, including General Maruyama's 2nd Divison and another division which was scheduled for New Guinea. The troop movement was already well under way. General Vandegrift had no way of knowing that, except from the vague messages of the coastwatchers. He had become the victim of time and distance in his eagerness to deal the Japanese a serious blow. The principle of the operation had been sound enough; it would be repeated successfully later. The problem was the misunderstanding of the logistics and the rate of travel through the jungle. Because of that lack of knowledge, the Matanikau adventure was the worst self-created disaster the marines had suffered on Guadalcanal.

Soon the Raiders and the other marines had an inkling of things to come. The Japanese began bringing in field artillery, and the guns began to fire. The marines promptly dubbed the Japanese artillery "Pistol Pete." They could not see these guns in their concealed positions on the other side of the Matanikau River, but they could hear them, and at Henderson Field the engineers could see what damage they wrought. There was not going to be any easy end to the fighting on Guadalcanal. In a way, it had just begun.

—10—

Change in Command

The new Japanese offensive at Guadalcanal was beginning to take an ominous shape. In mid-September it was apparent to Admiral Koga and General Hyukatake, the two area commanders of army and navy, that a greater degree of cooperation between their forces was necessary because the battle for Guadalcanal was shaping up as something quite different from anything the Japanese had faced before.

Until this time the areas of responsibility of army and navy had been clearly delineated. The army was responsible for all operations of troops on land. Malaya, the Dutch East Indies, the Philippines, had all been "army shows." But in the Solomons and at New Guinea the battle was on land and in the air and at sea. The Japanese still controlled the sea comfortably enough, but not the air. The Cactus Air Force was being augmented almost weekly. Its big problem was the paucity of gasoline and spare parts, but in spite of that the Americans, Australians, and New Zealanders flew and fought almost daily to keep the Japanese from taking Henderson Field.

So in mid-September the Japanese Imperial Army and the Imperial Navy concluded an agreement. First, the army would complete its reinforcement of Guadalcanal, adding at least a division of troops. When that was done, the army and navy would make a combined attack on the Americans and recapture Henderson Field. The navy would make a constant effort to keep the Allies from resupplying the troops on Guadalcanal.

"This is the decisive battle between Japan and the United States," said the orders of the Japanese troops reinforcing the island. "It is a battle in which the rise or fall of the Japanese empire will be decided. If we do not succeed in the occupation of these islands, no one should expect to return to Japan alive. . . ."*

The marines decided to make another attempt to wipe out the threat west of the Matanikau. The date chosen was October 8; the reasoning was that it might be possible to push the Japanese back before they got too many reinforcements on the island. And the reinforcements were already noticeable. In fact, on October 6 the Japanese moved the 4th Japanese Infantry regiment up to the west bank of the river. It was

---

* The order represented the usual hyperbole of the Japanese military, in which such terms as "annihilate," "crush," and "destroy" always bristled, but in this case the order was almost prophetic. Except for the men isolated and bypassed on islands, almost none of the fighters in the South Pacific ever did get home again. At the end of the fighting on Guadalcanal, the Japanese did stage a brilliant withdrawal movement. But after the Solomons campaign there were no more withdrawals. The garrisons of islands attacked fought to the death, island after island.

definitely a new threat to Henderson Field. General Maruyama had given Colonel Nakaguma his instructions. He had even named the place where General Vandegrift was to appear with a white flag to surrender on October 15, the day the "decisive battle" was to end in a Japanese victory.

The 1st Raider Battalion had gone into reserve. The men had been fighting very hard since August, and everyone recognized the fact. But the Japanese threat could not be ignored, and there were still not enough troops on the island to contain the Japanese properly. Plans had been made to send the 164th Infantry Regiment of the Army's Americal Division to Guadalcanal, but they had not yet arrived, and fresh Japanese troops were arriving every day. So the Raiders were pulled out of "rest camp." Colonel Edson ordered part of the battalion up front on the river on October 7. Company A and part of Company E moved, and that night bivouacked near Edson's command post.

Next morning just after dawn Major Walt of the 5th Marines took the Raiders and his own men toward the river. Company A stopped at the riverbank and put up barbed wire around the defensive position. The marines were expecting a Japanese attack at any time, one that would try to get through to Henderson Field. Company C came up a little later and joined the others of the 1st Raider Battalion.

Six battalions of marines were now preparing for an attack across the Matanikau River, but at the same time the Japanese were preparing to drive against Henderson Field from this point, as noted, and Colonel Nakaguma had brought his battalions up and was prepared to thrust across the river in two columns, one to move inland and the other to go along the beach. Some of the advance troops crossed the river on October 7 and ran into the marines. The Japanese were pushed back into a bend in the river, about a half mile from the mouth, and there they set up defensive positions, expecting the others of the force to cross over the next day.

On October 8 Colonel Edson ordered the men of Colonel Whaling's 3rd Battalion of the 2nd Marines to march upstream to Nippon Bridge. The Raiders were left behind to deal with this Japanese salient on their side of the river. But on October 8 the rain came down in sheets, forestalling any effective operations in the morning. In the afternoon the mud prevented an attack. But by nightfall the mud had dried a little. The Japanese staged a banzai attack that night; they charged in among the marines, and caused a number of casualties. They were finally stopped by the barbed wire and driven onto a sandspit in the river, where they were killed one by one.

By this time General Vandegrift realized that the Japanese had brought in many reinforcements and were not going to be easily contained and driven out of the Matanikau area. On October 8 Colonel Whaling got up the river, and on October 9 the troops crossed Nippon Bridge and marched down the west bank, unopposed and unseen. Behind them came the 2nd Battalion of the 7th Marines, and they went farther west and then cut down to Matanikau Village.

They saw no Japanese. Why not? Lieutenant Colonel Puller's 1st Battalion of the 7th Marines discovered why not. They crossed over Nippon Bridge behind the other two units and came down a trail half a mile west of the river, toward the coast. Suddenly, from the top of a ridge they looked down into two ravines, which were absolutely alive with Japanese troops. So confident had the Japanese been that there were no marines about, they had not maintained security. They were completely unaware of the enemy on the ridge. Colonel Puller radioed division headquarters and requested an artillery strike on one ravine. He began a mortar barrage on the other. The Japanese were surprised and they panicked, scrabbling up the sides of the ravines, and then being shot down by Puller's machine gunners and riflemen. The artillery boomed and the shells fell into the other ravine. The same scrabbling and panic ensued, and the Japanese were completely routed. After the battle—or the slaughter—the Japanese bodies were counted. There were 690 dead Japanese in the two ravines.

But down on the beach, the Japanese preparations for their offensive against Henderson Field continued. On October 9 General Hyukatake came personally to direct the campaign, and on October 11 there were preparations for the landing of a new Japanese supply force, this one bringing heavy artillery and reinforcements, tanks, and equipment with which the Japanese proposed to conquer Guadalcanal.

The Japanese continued to assemble. Every night more troops came down to Guadalcanal, each destroyer carrying 150 or more troops, discharging them off the northwestern end of the island, and then preparing to fight, or bombarding Henderson Field. At midnight on October 9 the cruiser *Tatsuta* and five destroyers landed General Hyukatake and his staff at Tassafaronga.

On October 11 the Japanese came back toward Guadalcanal, and from Rabaul, Admiral Junichi Kusaka, the commander of the 11th Air Fleet, sent a large force of bombers to "neutralize" Henderson Field, which they did. Admiral Mikawa then came down with a large contingent of ships, three cruisers and two destroyers, and two seaplane tenders and six destroyers carrying troops. The Americans and the Japanese fought the battle of Cape Esperance, which turned out to be an American victory in terms of ships sunk and damaged, but the Japanese managed to land men, supplies, and 150mm guns on Guadalcanal.

On the morning of October 13 the Americans landed from the transports, and the 164th Infantry reinforced the marines. Early on the morning of October 14 the Japanese brought battleships and cruisers down to bombard Henderson Field, and they did a good job. Of ninety planes on the field, they destroyed or damaged more than half. The field itself was unusable, and only a small fighter strip could land and take off planes. The situation looked desperate for the marines on Guadalcanal once more. And on the night of October 14, the last of General Hyukatake's reinforcing troops from Rabaul came down the slot to Guadalcanal in six transports. They landed at Tassafaronga, in full view of the Americans, and there was nothing the Americans could do to stop them. Henderson Field was completely unusable for the moment, and it had no gas. But by the next day some gasoline had been brought from Espiritu Santo, and that afternoon, flying from the fighter strip alongside, the Allied planes wrecked three of the Japanese transports, cutting to pieces the supplies they were bringing for General Hyukatake. Even so at this time, two months after the original marine landings on Guadalcanal, the American situation was so serious that Admiral Nimitz, known for his optimism, turned very gloomy.

"It now appears that we are unable to control the sea in the Guadalcanal area. Thus our supply of the positions will only be done at great expense to us. The situation is not hopeless, but it is extremely critical."

Faced with a new Japanese counterattack against Henderson Field, the Japanese ability to run destroyers, cruisers, and battleships and transports down the slot to reinforce Guadalcanal and to hit the marines, and the fact that the Allies could control the Guadalcanal air space only in the daylight hours, the marines were in their most desperate period.

Admiral Nimitz decided that something must be done. And he did it. He relieved Admiral Ghormley of command in the South Pacific and sent in Admiral William F. Halsey, his most belligerent "fighting admiral." Admiral Halsey was now given the responsibility for turning uncertainty into victory.

—11—

The Long March of
the 2nd Raiders

The Raiders had been brought over from Tulagi early
in August to save Henderson Field, and here they were
back again, two months later, though not on the same
line, doing the same thing. The difference was that this
time the Japanese had a division of troops to fight, not
just three battalions.

But the Raiders finally got a break. It resulted from
a dispute between the navy and the Marine Corps
about Raiders in general. Admiral Richmond Kelly
Turner was very much impressed with the 1st Raider
Battalion's performance in the early fighting on Guadalcanal. Every marine unit ought to have a Raider
battalion, said Admiral Turner. And he set about im-
plementing the idea in his own command. He had
control of 1,400 marines of the 2nd Marine Regiment.
He decided that he would train them as Raiders before
sending them into action. This decision was not made

known immediately to General Vandegrift, who was calling loudly in September for reinforcements. He wanted marines, and he wanted them fast, and he did not want to wait while Kelly Turner trained them more than they needed. Turner paid no attention, but announced that he would train Raider battalions for the 7th and 8th Marines, who were under his command just then. Everybody from Admiral Ghormley to Admiral Nimitz had warned against it. Finally the commandant of the Marine Corps got into the fracas, and pointed out to Admiral Turner that he, Lieutenant General Thomas Holcomb, commanded the U. S. Marine Corps, not Admiral Turner, and that there already was a 2nd Raider Battalion which just then was being sent to General Vandegrift in response to his call for reinforcements.

In this argument the name of Raider loomed very high, and someone finally paid some attention to the needs of the 1st Raider Battalion, which was worn out after two months of the most strenuous effort. The 1st Raiders were packed off to Noumea for rest. They needed it. Colonel Edson was gone. Colonel Griffith was wounded in the shoulder and out of action. Major Bailey was dead. The men were yellow with Atabrine, which only suppressed their malaria. And General Vandegrift agreed that the unit had to be rebuilt and restored to health before he could use them effectively again. So they were marched aboard the transport *Zeitlin* and sent to New Caledonia, cheering.

Now, early in October, General Hyukatake was in personal command of the Japanese assault forces for Guadalcanal, and he was preparing for the big battle, after which he would plant the "red meatball" or *hinamaru* flag on Henderson Field. The date of the attack was set for October 22. The land forces would strike for Henderson Field, the air forces from Rabaul would come down in strong support, the naval forces of the Combined Fleet would bombard from offshore and be prepared to annihilate the American fleet if it should appear.

General Hitoshi Imamura, the newly appointed area commander, and General Hyukatake completely underestimated the number of American troops on Guadalcanal; they believed there might be as many as 7,500 when actually there were 16,000 marines and soldiers on the island. The Japanese took the problem seriously: they assigned four generals to the operation. General Hyukatake assigned Major General Tadashi Sumiyoshi to attack the marine positions on the Matanikau River. Major General Kawaguchi, who knew the terrain, was to strike on the left side of Henderson Field. Major General Yumio Nasu was to strike with a brigade on the western side of Henderson Field. Lieutenant General Masai Maruyama, commander of the 2nd Division, was to coordinate these attacks. So the Japanese certainly had plenty of brass allocated to the recapture of Guadalcanal. And after October 15, every night the Tokyo Express came down to the island, bringing more troops, about a thousand a night.

Although the major assault on Henderson Field was set for October 22, two days earlier General Sumiyoshi struck the marines on the Matanikau River, and Colonel McKelvy's battalion. The battle began with heavy mortar and artillery fire from the Japanese side. The next morning nine tanks tried to cross the river on the coast road, but they were battered by the marine artillery until they either were destroyed or turned back.

Then came the assault day, October 22, but because of the problems of the navy in preparing for a fleet battle, the major combined effort was delayed. That day the destroyer *Nicholas* got into a battle with one of the Japanese shore batteries that was firing on a transport the *Nicholas* had just escorted to Lunga Roads. The *Nicholas* fired one thousand rounds of five-inch ammunition and the battery was silenced at least temporarily.

On October 23 General Sumiyoshi started again against the positions of the marines and other troops on the Matanikau River, but the 105mm howitzers of the marine artillery destroyed twelve tanks, and the marines stopped the infantry attack. On October 24 another element of Japanese suddenly appeared upstream on the Matanikau, and the 3rd Battalion of the 7th Marines was rushed up with artillery support to cover. The Japanese now also had their own artillery support west of the Matanikau, sixteen big guns firing fourteen-inch shells.

For the next three days the Japanese in great force struck the marine lines, which bent but never broke, and despite naval bombardment and aerial bombardment and constant ground attack, the marines triumphed and held Henderson Field. They repulsed attacks at Matanikau, at Hannken's Ridge, and at a position half a mile south of Bloody Ridge called Coffin Corner. The Japanese had lost thousands killed—950 Japanese were buried at Coffin Corner alone after one day's fighting. The marines lost 182 men killed and the 164th Infantry lost 166 killed and wounded.

* * *

By mid-November the Japanese attack had been blunted in the air, on the sea, and on the land. The 1st Marine Division, which had been fighting for fifteen weeks, was sent to join the Raiders for rest and reorganization. The 8th Marines came to Guadalcanal. The 6th Marines and the 182nd Army Infantry were on their way.

General Vandegrift wanted to push westward now and wipe out the Japanese. An attenuated battle at Point Cruz in mid-November proved that the Japanese were not beaten yet. And while this was going on, Lieutenant Colonel Carlson's 2nd Raider Battalion was brought into actions on Guadalcanal.

The 2nd Raiders had been having it easy for a while. They had returned from the Makin raid to spend a week in the luxury of the Royal Hawaiian Hotel on Waikiki Beach in Honolulu. Steak and fruit and ice cream every night. Clean sheets too. Then it had been a trip to Espiritu Santo by ship, and some more training.

Admiral Turner got the idea that he wanted to build a new airfield at Aola Bay, on Guadalcanal, fifty miles east of Lunga Point. Admiral Halsey thought it was a fine idea. Nobody consulted General Vandegrift, who knew the terrain and knew that Aola Point was an impossible site for an airfield. The first Vandegrift knew of the plan was when an army infantry regiment showed up with a battalion of Seabees, and the 2nd Raider Battalion, with orders to go in to Aola Bay.

From Vandegrift's viewpoint it was a foolish idea. But there the Raiders and the others were, riding in aboard the old four-stack destroyers on November 4. When Colonel Carlson was shown his part of the job—establish the perimeter, defend it, secure it, and turn it over to the army—he saw it as so simple that he wanted to use only two companies of his battalion, so they boarded the destroyers along with the other members of the team and were off. They landed at Aola Bay without any opposition because there weren't any Japanese there.

The weather was rainy again. The tropical downpour drenched the Raiders as they hit the beach. And there they waited, soaking wet, for the landing craft to come back and get them. There was nothing for them to do. Very soon a plane appeared in the sky, an American plane, and it circled and waggled its wings, and ultimately dropped a message for Colonel Carlson. The message was from General Vandegrift: he had gainful employment for the Raider battalion. Vandegrift had learned that seventeen Japanese destroyers had just landed an entire new Japanese regiment at Kimimba and Tassafaronga to reinforce the Japanese who were attacking Henderson Field. Apparently General Hyukatake had reconsidered his opinion that there were not more than 7,500 Americans on the island.

The Raiders were to join the fight. They were to travel through the upper valley of the Tenaru River, and the upper Lunga River, make a detour around Mount Austen, which was crawling with Japanese, and come against the rear of the new Japanese regiment. When Lieutenant Colonel Carlson learned this, he wrote out a request for the dispatch of the rest of his battalion, Company B and Company E. They should be landed at some point on the coast where they could join the rest of the force.

The destroyers *McKean* and *Manley* went off without the Raiders, and they prepared to march across the island to attack the Japanese from the rear. Major John Mather of the Australian Army was with them, and he had a detachment of native scouts who would lead the Raiders across the island, through the jungle, to get at the Japanese. They had not brought much food with them, expecting to be resupplied by the destroyers. But now they would have to make do until they could receive supplies.

At dawn on November 6 they marched. The native scouts set out first to hack a trail through the jungle. Then along came the Raiders and the native carriers, who were lugging the food and ammunition for the party. During the training period Carlson had told the men that they might find themselves in a situation where if they wanted to eat they would have to discover the enemy and take the food from him. The warning was now coming true. And so they marched, the scouts and then the Raiders, five paces apart, with Lieutenant Colonel Carlson near the front of the line, gnawing on the smelly black pipe that was a part of him, and sometimes smoking it if the conditions were right. The middle-aged Carlson was carrying a full pack, just like his boys, following his principle that he would not ask them to do anything he would not do himself. There was another Carlson along on this mission too. Lieutenant Evans C. Carlson, the colonel's son, who had been trying to get into the Raiders for months but had just recently managed to secure the colonel's permission, after the colonel was sure that the youngster could do everything the others could do, and for the most part better than the others.

Carlson and Major Mather had plotted their route on a map: it led through the villages of Gegende, Reko, Tasimboko, Tina, and Binu. Major Mather had selected the route because his intelligence said that all these villages had been either occupied or visited by the Japanese within the past few days.

Each Raider carried a four-day supply of food in his pack, and that was all there was. If they ate it all in two days, they would go hungry. Carlson had arranged for a tenuous supply system, the best he could manage. They were to depend on the army and the Seabees back at Aola. A four-day supply of food was to be standard; Carlson would be in touch with Aola by radio, and the base was to dispatch a landing craft loaded with food to a prearranged point along the beach. Carlson would then send off a patrol with carriers, to pick up the food.

They marched by day and rested by night. Late in the afternoon they would bivouac and the men would prepare their food: rice and bacon, raisins, chocolate, and tea. These were iron rations laced with salt, and that was all. After eating, the men would douse the small fires and then wrap up in their ponchos for protection against the rain, and sleep a few hours.

There were no Japanese at Gegende, although there were signs that the enemy had been there. But the Raiders made contact with the enemy at the village of Reko. A native scout was leading the column as they approached the village, which was located on a small river on the edge of the jungle. The Japanese saw him and opened fire. The scout went down, shot in both arms. Raiders slipped past him, spotted the gray-green uniforms of Japanese troops, and opened fire. Five Japanese had been in the village, and now they fled, but two of them did not move fast enough and they were shot down. That small patrol was the only indication of the enemy so far.

They moved on to Tasimboko. There were no Japanese here, in this village that had once been a stronghold. They marched to Tina, and still found no Japanese. On November 9 they marched on to Binu, still found no enemy troops, but did find at Binu a messenger from General Vandegrift. The Japanese had landed near the Metapona River and there they had been trapped in a pocket by marine and army troops. But it was a big pocket, and no one knew how many Japanese were in there. General Vandegrift wanted Carlson and his Raiders to make contact and find out so General Vandegrift would know how many men to send.

Carlson decided that Binu would be their base of operations, so the men unslung their packs. The Japanese in the pocket were just three miles away. From here the Raiders could secure intelligence about Japanese activity and they could cover the Japanese flanks and rear in case they tried an attack against the marines and army on the other side.

Carlson spent the first day interviewing villagers through Major Mather's interpretation. On November 10 he sent a patrol of Raiders to get in touch with the 2nd Battalion of the 7th Marines. Colonel Hanneken reported that the Japanese were indeed enclosed in a pocket, as reported, although they were full of fight.

Back at Binu, Lieutenant Colonel Carlson made his plans. Next day they would attack. The irony, that the next day was November 11, the day of the signing of peace in World War I, was not lost on the Raiders. There would be no armistice in this war, and they knew it. It had been part of Colonel Carlson's training program to teach the Raiders that they were fighting for unconditional surrender of a tough enemy.

That day the Raiders of Company B and Company E joined up with the column at Binu. They had been landed at Tasimboko and had marched overland. So Carlson had his full force. The next day, he decided, he would send out patrols to search for the enemy. Each patrol would carry its own radio and keep in touch with the battalion command post by calling in every two hours. When one patrol found the enemy, all the units would be brought to that point to make a concentrated attack. This was another bit of borrowing from the Chinese communist system of guerrilla warfare; Mao Zedong's concept was that small enemy units should be cut off, enveloped, and destroyed. One company would remain at Binu to maintain the base and provide a rear guard and a reserve.

It was raining again, another tropical outburst of the monsoon season, and the cooking fires smoked and smoldered and the smoke hung heavy in the air of the village. But this was of no matter here, because the Japanese would expect the Binu villagers to have cooking fires.

On November 11 Lieutenant Colonel Carlson sent his four scouting companies out. Company C went west to Asamana village on the Metapona River. The natives had reported a large contingent of Japanese soldiers there.

Company E moved north to explore a trail begun by the native scouts. Company D would then move past Company E and go farther north to meet the 164th U.S. Army Infantry. Company F went northeast to patrol between the American lines and the Balesuma

River. Lieutenant Colonel Carlson remained at the command post in Binu, with Company A, which could be quickly moved to any point if it was needed.

At ten o'clock in the morning Company E reported in. A large force of Japanese might be moving on Binu, they said. They had learned from the 7th Marines that several hundred Japanese had escaped a trap set for them the day before and had come through the lines, moving south. They might be coming toward the Raiders.

At ten minutes after ten that morning, Company C checked in. They had found those Japanese, they said. They were set up nearby, armed with machine guns, mortars, and 20mm antivehicle guns. Action was about to begin for the 2nd Raider Battalion on Guadalcanal.

—12—

The Perimeter of
Henderson Field

On Armistice Day 1943, Lieutenant Colonel Evans Carlson prepared his Raiders for a fight. He moved Company E south, along the bank of the Metapona River. From here the Raiders were to cross the river at Samana and attack the Japanese on the flank, about a mile east of the village.

Company D would move up to make a frontal assault on the enemy, who were dug in in a woody area. Company C reported that it had found the enemy and was about to attack, so Carlson sent part of Company A to help them and called Company F back to the command post to go into reserve. By eleven A.M. the movement was in process.

Half an hour later Company E announced that it was about to attack at Asamana. The company commander said he had spotted about two companies of Japanese as they were moving across the river.

Lieutenant Colonel Carlson waited for results. The men of Company F arrived, exhausted from a forced march to return to base. Carlson told them to eat and rest, and then be prepared to move out again when the time came.

Native scouts arrived to report on the enemy. The Japanese had split their force. The smaller part of it was at Asamana, about to be engaged by Company E. The larger force was going somewhere, either to strike the 7th Marines in a flanking movement or to head for Henderson Field. From the direction in which they were moving it could be either, and Carlson did not care much, for he had decided to attack and destroy this force. Company C had already engaged them and stopped them three miles away.

Carlson did not know it, but Company C's commander had blundered and the company was in serious trouble. In his eager pursuit of the enemy, the commander had been less than cautious. The company had been moving swiftly across an open field, too close behind the point—the scouts. The scouts had entered a wooded area, and stumbled there on the Japanese force, which was bivouacked for a rest. The Japanese leapt for their weapons, and the American scouts dropped to the ground and began firing. But behind them out in the open was the rest of the company with virtually no cover. The Japanese recovered from their surprise and opened fire on the field. Those 20mm dual-purpose guns and the machine guns began to cut away at the cover of the marines. The captain got his mortars into action, but the Japanese were using their grenade launchers with their usual efficiency and so the mortars had to change position after firing one or two shells. After an hour of fighting, the Japanese had lost twenty-four men, most of them in the surprise in the beginning, and the Raiders had lost five men killed and three wounded. They moved back out of the field, set up a perimeter, and engaged the Japanese at long range with mortar fire. At 3:30 that afternoon, when the men of Company F had rested for a while, Lieutenant Colonel Carlson led them out to find Company C and engage the enemy. They marched briskly for an hour, and then Carlson found Company C, completely disorganized, with the command post much too far behind the line to be effective. The action had settled down to a desultory exchange of mortar fire.

Carlson was thoroughly disgusted with Company C. He put the company in reserve, called up Company E to come from Asamana, where it had routed the Japanese, and he prepared to attack with Company F. First he called Henderson Field and asked for an air strike on the Japanese in the woods beyond the big open field. Then he moved into a finger of woods, and an hour after Carlson's arrival he was attacking. But the Japanese were gone, leaving a handful of snipers to harry the attacking marines.

At dusk two dive bombers arrived, circled, and attacked the woods beyond the open field. They dropped bombs and came back to strafe. Lieutenant Colonel Carlson then sent a squad across the field. The Raiders made no contact with the enemy; they were all gone. It was growing dark very fast, so Carlson called a halt to the attack. Since he was not familiar with the ground, he set up a perimeter and left F Company. He took Company C back to Binu, where Company E and Company D had already arrived. The casualties were tended, and the tired marines settled down to sleep.

Lieutenant Colonel Carlson sat up late, solving some serious problems. The commanders of Company C and Company D had both failed the test of leadership that day, and under the Raider system developed by Lieutenant Colonel Carlson, the men had told him so. The commander of Company C had caused five men to get killed by his carelessness. The commander of Company D had failed in almost the same way. After Company D had made contact with the enemy, the company commander had made the mistake of moving out with his point men, in a show of bravery, and had lost contact with the main elements of the company when the point came under fire and was pinned down. Two Raiders were killed and one was wounded before the point could get away from the hail of fire. When they got back to the company, they found it disorganized, and they did not engage the enemy again that day.

So Lieutenant Colonel Carlson made the tough decision. The two company commanders were relieved, which meant they were lost as far as effectiveness in any job was concerned. This was very hard for Carlson, because he took the responsibility; he had supervised the training of these officers and he had failed. Also, the failures of the day had set back their whole plan of attack and all that would have to be rectified.

On November 12 Carlson took a patrol to the scene of Company C's battle with the Japanese to find out what he could about the movement of the enemy. The Japanese had left their dead behind, and there might be papers on the bodies to give him some information. He discovered that Company F's commander had already been doing some scouting. He had learned that the Japanese had crossed the Metapona River the previous night and had gotten clean away.

The Raiders buried the dead, sticking the dog tags and helmets of the marines on top of the rude crosses so that the graves registration people could find them later and identify the bodies. They waited while Company D and Company E came up from Binu, and then Carlson moved out with these companies, sending Company F back to Binu to join Company C as a reserve. On the river they encountered a pair of Japanese in a boat and killed them. Near Asamana they found three more Japanese stragglers and killed them too.

At Asamana Carlson found a bivouac that had housed at least a battalion of Japanese. This was a staging area not far from Henderson Field, and an excellent site for preparing for an attack. That was what he wanted to know—just how large was the force he was following. It seemed to be a permanent camp. There were notices pinned to trees, telling various units where to set up. And there was other evidence of some permanence—slit trenches, latrines, and campfire sites. Carlson did not have long to contemplate all this, for firing broke out. A Japanese unit had arrived at the bivouac site from the river.

Lieutenant Colonel Carlson called Binu on his radio and told the operator to send Company C to join him. He set up a perimeter then, and planned to ambush the Japanese as they came into the bivouac area.

All day long small units of Japanese kept showing up to walk into the trap. By day's end the Raiders had killed twenty-six Japanese soldiers, including one officer. When darkness came, the marines set up their perimeter again, and settled down. The night was quiet, but the next morning Carlson discovered that the Japanese knew they were in the bivouac and had set up in the woods around them, preparing to attack.

Lieutenant Colonel Carlson called for artillery support from the guns at Henderson Field. Soon the shells were falling in the woods on the north, west, and south sides of the Raiders as he had asked. The marines were on the watch for enemy activity, but they saw nothing. Then one Raider saw movement, but he could not figure out what it was. The underbrush seemed to be moving into the clearing in front of the marines. The marines called for the colonel, who came up and looked through his field glasses. He knew then what the Japanese were doing. Each Japanese soldier had camouflaged himself with branches, and they were moving up as a skirmish line, ever so slowly, to surprise the marines. So Carlson passed the word along the line. The marines were to wait until the Japanese had come close, and then they were to mow them down.

So the line of brush kept moving up, until it was only a hundred yards from the marines. Then the Raiders opened fire with machine guns, Garand rifles, and Browning automatic rifles. The line of brush disintegrated, and individual bushes went staggering back to the Japanese line.

The Japanese continued the tactic all day long, and five times the marines lay in wait and then ambushed the incoming Japanese skirmish line. At the end of the day the Raiders in their foxholes waited nervously for a night banzai charge, but it never came. They did hear naval gunfire that night. The Tokyo Express had come down again, this time including the battleships

Hiei and *Kirishima*. The Japanese won another naval victory that night, sinking two American cruisers and four destroyers. But the Japanese did not have time to bombard Henderson Field, and so an attack that was planned had not come off. The Japanese did bombard Henderson the next day, November 13, and landed more reinforcing troops from transports. But seven transports were sunk that day and the Japanese plans received a serious setback. The Americans lost eighteen planes in the bombardment of Henderson Field, but the attack did not come off.

On November 14 Carlson took stock. His Raiders were very tired after so many forced marches. Worse, they were hungry. They had been moving so fast the food supply could not keep up with them. On this day Carlson had been waiting at Binu for resupply. That meant he could not move out because there were not enough native carriers to move the food around. Carlson planted the men at Binu to await the carriers, and then he went on a scouting mission of his own. He went to the village of Volinivua, which was the command post of the 7th Marines, and he conferred with them about the next steps the Raiders should take. It was agreed that they would move up to Asamana and patrol south from there for a few days.

Carlson went back to join the Raiders for the night, and the next morning he was up early, talking to Major Mather about the Japanese. Mather's scouts reported the Japanese in some force in a valley about five miles south of Binu. How many? That was always a problem because of the limited arithmetical skills of the Solomon Islanders. So Carlson sent Captain Schwerin of F Company with a patrol to find out. Schwerin and his men crawled up the ridge to look down into the valley.

There they saw a sentry on the side of their hill and Japanese moving about below. Schwerin considered the problem. The sentry posed a real obstacle. If they killed him, they would run the possibility of raising the alarm, and the others would undoubtedly get away. Captain Schwerin waited. Then he had an idea, learned from Carlson about the Japanese. They almost always ate together. So the captain waited. In late afternoon the Japanese began to boil up their rice. When it was cooked, they called the sentry, as Schwerin had hoped they would, and he left his post and went into camp. Then the Raiders began to move. In groups of three they crawled down the hill and surprised the Japanese at their dinner. There were fifteen of them, and the Raiders killed them all in a few bursts of fire. Then they picked up usable guns, ammunition, food, and documents, and took them back with them to Binu. The documents were turned over to the interpreters, and the marines feasted on the food the patrol had brought back. They had not lost a man.

—13—

The End of "Pistol Pete"

In the middle of November 1943, Carlson's Raiders were at Asamana hunting down stragglers from the main Japanese force supposedly trapped in that pocket by the army and the 7th Marines. But nearly all the Japanese had escaped by swimming across the Malimbiu River in small groups and had marched up to the hills on the west.

There really was nothing for the Raiders to do there, so after two days of fruitless patrol, Lieutenant Colonel Carlson traveled to General Vandegrift's headquarters to consult about new orders.

Yes, said General Vandegrift, there was a mission that would make use of the peculiar talents of the Raiders. "Pistol Pete," the big artillery piece the Japanese had brought to Guadalcanal, was still giving the men of Henderson Field trouble. The Raiders could take on the task of wiping out "Pistol Pete."

So Lieutenant Colonel Carlson prepared for the new job. The first problem, he knew from experience, was to arrange for supplies while on the trail. On the last mission his boys had gone hungry too much of the time, and their ammunition supply had nearly given out at one point. To prevent that, Carlson went out by himself, scouted the area they were going to traverse, and found suitable campsites. He marked them all on his map, and then went back to headquarters to confer with the supply people and the air force. There he found an additional project. He was to try to locate the trail the Japanese had used to travel from the Lunga River area to the Matanikau River, so the marines could prevent its use in reverse.

Once again Lieutenant Colonel Carlson took a page from the book of Mao Zedong. To find "Pistol Pete" he was going to have to secure some good intelligence. He began by questioning the native scouts, but this was not much help, because to the Solomon Islanders one field piece looked like another, and so several of the scouts described guns to him. They might be 20mm guns or 155mm, he had no way of knowing. He decided to find out by trial and error. He would send out a number of small patrols, and when one patrol located the gun or guns, he would throw the entire strength of the Raider battalion against that point.

So the men of the battalion began to move out on their intelligence missions. Carlson moved the command post to a point on the upper Tenaru River. Company A, which had been held at Espiritu Santo, now joined up, bringing the battalion to full strength for the first time since the beginning of the Guadalcanal struggle.

Carlson divided the battalion into two combat

124

groups. One set up a command post two miles to the right of the battalion headquarters. The other set up two miles to the left. The scout units began searching for trails and soon found two well-used trails that the marines had not known about. Then, on the night of November 28, Captain Schwerin's scouts found the site of one of the big pieces of artillery. The gun was gone, but some ammunition for the 155mm gun remained. The Raiders destroyed it.

Another scout team went to the village of Andu on the Tenaru River, and there found another new trail, which led to the Lunga area. It was so heavily traveled that Carlson decided it must be the main trail to the Japanese central garrison. So on the morning of November 29 Carlson led the whole battalion out along that trail and into the Lunga valley. The terrain there was even rougher than most of Guadalcanal; in places the only way up the slope was by the use of mountain-climbing techniques and ropes. The top was a natural artillery-spotter's position, overlooking Henderson Field and the Lunga Point area. There they found a bivouac and a telephone line that went down the western side of the mountain. They traced the line down the mountain until they came to a flat plain, and there was the big gun and a smaller field piece. There was ammunition, but there were no Japanese around the artillery. Once again scouts went out, and they found another bivouac. The Raiders ambushed this bivouac, flushed out five Japanese soldiers, and killed them.

The battalion stopped here, but Company F went ahead to scout. It began to rain, and soon a tropical downpour enveloped the area. One patrol emerged from the brush and blundered into the enemy. They found a large Japanese party, arms neatly stacked in a clearing, the men huddled under trees to escape the rain. The marines dropped, and opened fire with Garand rifles and Browning automatic rifles. The Japanese scattered. The marines brought up machine guns and began spattering the area with fire. Only then did they realize that they had suprised an entire platoon, and before long they had killed most of the Japanese, who never were able to get at their weapons.

When the action was over, the marines counted seventy-five dead Japanese.

The next day was spent waiting for supplies at the command post on the Tenaru. Lieutenant Colonel Carlson and the interpreters checked the documents and papers they found on the Japanese bodies for intelligence about the enemy's operations. When the rain finally stopped, the men tried to dry out their clothes.

A big cargo plane from Henderson Field appeared and dropped supplies by parachute into the clearing where the Raiders had set out cloth panels. The Douglas DC-3 made seven trips that day. Some of the supplies fell into the Tenaru River and were lost. Some fell in the jungle, and Lieutenant Colonel Carlson cautioned the men against going in to retrieve them. The jungle was alive with Japanese, and anyone who ventured in was in danger. One Raider who did not heed Carlson's advice was killed by a sniper that day. But the others paid attention, and they managed to collect about three quarters of the supplies dropped to them.

As far as General Vandegrift was concerned, the Raiders had accomplished their mission with the capture of "Pistol Pete" and he ordered them to return to headquarters. But Lieutenant Colonel Carlson felt that he was about to come to grips with a major Japanese unit, and he asked permission to delay the return for a few days. It was granted.

The Raiders were on the plain, at the foot of Mount Mombula, a 1,500-foot peak that stands above Henderson Field. The mountain was then held by the Japanese, and Carlson felt that he might rectify that situation. He sent out many patrols again, trying to find the location of the main enemy group. One patrol found the barrel of a gun and wrecked that. Another patrol moved into the Lunga valley and found a Japanese patrol. The Raiders got into a firefight with the Japanese and killed ten of them without losing a man. Still another patrol went up the south side of Mount Mombula. They made the wearying trip to the top, and there found a Japanese position, well dug in, overlooking Henderson Field. But there were no Japanese around the top of Mount Mombula.

The patrol returned to the command post to report to Lieutenant Colonel Carlson. When he had this information he made his plan. He would march part of the battalion to the top of Mount Mombula, destroy the Japanese position, and then march down the mountain to Henderson Field, destroying any other camps as he went and eliminating any Japanese.

In the fashion of leadership that Carlson had developed, he talked his plans over with the men. They were a sorry lot by this time; of the six hundred men of the battalion, one fourth had malaria and about thirty had dysentery. Most of them had ringworm or jungle rot, and all but Company A were tired and dirty from a solid month in the jungle. Carlson selected three companies to go with him over Mount Mombula. Company A he chose because it was the freshest. Company B and Company F he chose because they had performed best in the past. Company D and Company C would go back to camp the way they had come. They would be led by Captain Washburn of Company E because the other two companies had only temporary commanders following Lieutenant Colonel Carlson's relief of the incompetent commanders when they were at Binu.

The companies formed up into two columns and set out, going their separate ways, all singing "Onward, Christian Soldiers," which must have given the Japanese lurking in the jungle a considerable surprise.

Captain Washburn marched his troops back to the Tenaru River and along its banks until he reached the Lunga Roads area and the main marine base. There were no incidents. They did not encounter any Japanese.

Lieutenant Colonel Carlson led his men up the steep, slippery slopes of Mount Mombula. It was raining again, and the slopes of the mountain were slippery with mud and slick grass. The Raiders panted their way up the mountain, grasping at shrubs and roots to help them climb through the clay mud. Finally they neared the summit. Lieutenant Colonel Carlson paused. He had just seen some fresh Japanese footprints. They all stopped and he motioned for quiet. He called up Lieutenant Jack Miller and instructed him to push forward very quietly to the crest of the hill with a patrol. They went off, and the rest of the Raiders moved up slowly and silently until they found a position suitable for an ambush. They stopped there and waited.

Fifteen minutes went by with no action. Then a Japanese patrol suddenly appeared on the trail from above and started into the trap. But their leader was war-wise, and he suddenly sensed that something was very much wrong. He shouted, and all the Japanese dropped off the trail and into the brush alongside. Their gray-green uniforms made them extremely difficult to see. They opened fire. The marines opened fire with their Garands and automatic weapons. Three Japanese were killed, but the others—Carlson was not quite sure how many there were—continued to fight.

This was a very large Japanese patrol, and it was equipped with machine guns and mortars as well as rifles. The mortars and the "knee mortars," or grenade launchers, were the most formidable weapons in this jungle terrain. Carlson told his men to knock them out first if they could. The Raiders began looking for mortarmen, and sharpshooting. Carlson then ordered a double envelopment, and squads went out to each flank to carry out the order. Captain Gary, commander of Company A, controlled the flankers. But then the Japanese decided to outflank the Americans. This change posed a serious question. It would take more than a squad or two to change the picture. So Carlson sent a full platoon out to left and right, and they moved out far enough to avoid the enemy, and then came together in his rear. Now the marines had the Japanese in a vise. But that did not mean the Japanese were beaten. They continued to fight fiercely. A number of them had taken cover down in a ravine in the center of the line, and Carlson sent BAR men down to hit them from both flanks and flush them out. The other marines moved up cautiously, checking every bit of ground as they went, and flushed out more Japanese, and killed them.

In the rear of the Japanese, Lieutenant Miller was wounded by bullets from a .45-caliber Thompson sub-machine gun that the Japanese had captured earlier. Several slugs had hit him, and they had made serious wounds, much worse than those of the .25-caliber bullets from the Nambu rifles the Japanese usually carried.

At the end of two hours of fighting, three other Raiders were wounded. But twenty-five dead Japanese lay on the side of the mountain. There were no sounds from the jungle. All the others had slipped away.

The marines were exhausted from the climb and the fight, and it was too late to continue to move up the mountain, so they made camp. They had no water nor did they build fires. They ate cold rations and tended the wounded. Lieutenant Miller had a very bad night. He needed medical attention immediately, but there was no way for him to get it.

The next morning the marines started down the Henderson Field side of the mountain. The going was just as rough going down as it had been on the other side going up. B Company led the way and walked into an ambush. The Japanese were concealed in the trees and the jungle alongside the trail. Before the marines could start shooting back, Raider Stephen Van Buren was mortally wounded. Several other Raiders were hit. The stretcher bearers stopped, put down their wounded, and took up their rifles. The Japanese tried their flanking technique again, but once more Lieutenant Colonel Carlson sent an entire platoon around behind the enemy and routed them out of the area. The fighting was very fierce, and two more Raiders were killed and two more were wounded. When the shooting stopped, Lieutenant Colonel Carlson investigated. He found seven dead Japanese, all in concealed positions. They had been left as a rear guard, and they had fought to the death. That was sobering enough; more sobering to Lieutenant Colonel Carlson was the news that Lieutenant Miller had died during this last fight. So they stopped there in the jungle on the side of the mountain and buried the marine dead, once more erecting rude crosses of branches and hanging the helmets and dog tags on them. Lieutenant Colonel Carlson said a prayer.

Having had this encounter with the rear guard, Lieutenant Colonel Carlson went forward as the march was resumed. He expected an encounter with the main Japanese force at any time, and the Raiders moved cautiously and watchfully. They did not encounter any Japanese, however, and when they came to a fork in the trail, Lieutenant Colonel Carlson thought he knew why. One portion of the trail led toward Henderson Field, but the other portion led off to the west. Carlson was sure that if he followed that trail, he would find the Japanese camp. But he could not follow the trail: He had orders from the general to return to base. So, reluctantly, Carlson led his Raiders back along the trail toward Henderson Field and soon entered the division's lines, and passed the challenge of a sentry. They were not far from the Matanikau River. They stopped at a command post and got transportation for the wounded to the base hospital, and then they marched another eight miles to their old bivouac on the Tenaru River. Lieutenant Colonel Carlson went to

131

division headquarters to see General Vandegrift, returned, and spent the next few days writing a report of the Raiders' exploits in the jungle.

The Raiders had killed nearly five hundred Japanese troops. They had lost sixteen men killed and eighteen wounded. They had captured "Pistol Pete" and several other field pieces and a number of Japanese rifles, which they gave to the Solomon Islands scouts. They had learned a good deal about jungle fighting, including the fact that their rations were not suitable for this sort of warfare. The standard field ration in those days was the tinned C ration, which was too bulky. Carlson suggested that a new sort of ration be developed, and it was. Soon the troops in the field had K rations, lightweight and small in bulk. A man could carry half a dozen K rations without much trouble, and that meant food for three days on his person.

The Raiders had learned a great deal about the Japanese, information that would be valuable in the island war. They now knew that the Japanese usually stuck to a single plan and were inflexible in it. If the plan could be unraveled, the Japanese tended to dissolve in confusion. They also learned that the Japanese fought to the death, and that it was no good trying to help a wounded Japanese, because more likely than not he would try to kill you even if it meant blowing himself and you up with a grenade.

Carlson had learned again something he knew from China, that the Japanese were easy to outflank, and that they were careless about their bivouacs and camps; they did not post enough guards.

The Raiders had also learned that while the Japanese were tenacious fighters, they were not the supermen that Japanese propaganda had proclaimed them to be and that the rush of events of the first days of the war had indicated. The myth of Japanese invincibility had been punctured in the Guadalcanal jungle.

Carlson's Raiders were relieved and sent down to Wellington, New Zealand, for a rest. They hoped they would have thirty days leave. But after a week they were suddenly shipped back to Espiritu Santo. Admiral Richmond Kelly Turner and Admiral Halsey had decided that they needed the Raiders for some new action that was being contemplated as the battle for Guadalcanal slowed down. In fact, the whole idea of the Raider battalions was under discussion. Admiral Turner was enormously enthusiastic about the Raiders and favored the establishment of several Raider regiments. Not all the Marine Corps officers liked the idea. They continued to believe that the Marine Corps was a unique striking force, and to have a special unit of shock troops within the corps disturbed them. But the idea was to get its trial, and very soon.

So the Raiders assembled at Espiritu Santo along with the 1st Raiders. The war correspondents had a field day with Carlson's Raiders, largely because of his Chinese background and the gung ho slogan of the 2nd Raider Battalion. After the Makin raid they had become celebrated, and now the 2nd Raider Battalion became the most highly publicized unit in the Marine Corps. Many medals were given out, including a third Navy Cross for Lieutenant Colonel Carlson, and a unit citation for the 2nd Raider Battalion. Back in Hollywood the moviemakers decided to make a film about Carlson's Raiders as a morale booster for the nation.

And the Raiders waited for orders. They were not too long in coming.

—14—

Moving North

At the end of 1942, Japan's Imperial General Head-quarters in Tokyo assessed the military situation in the Pacific. The Allies would try to move up the Solomon Islands, Imperial General Headquarters warned its various commands. Then they would attack Rabaul, the major army, navy, and air force base for the Japanese. After that they would move along the northern coast of New Guinea, and attack the Philippines.

That forecast turned out to be almost correct. As the fighting on Guadalcanal ceased, Admiral William F. Halsey was making plans at Noumea for an attack on New Georgia. This was to be the next step in the move toward Rabaul, and among other things it would pin down the Japanese fleet in the South Pacific, which was just where Admiral King wanted it to be while he carried the navy's drive across the Central Pacific toward Japan.

By February the Americans were ready to move again. Admiral Halsey set April as the time for the invasion of New Georgia. The Raider battalions were warned that they would be playing a role in this campaign. So they were going to continue operations in the Solomons, an area the marine historians could characterize only as hot, humid, and unhealthy.

With the close of the Guadalcanal campaign the 1st and 2nd Raider battalions were shipped first to Wellington, New Zealand, and then back to Noumea. Lieutenant Colonel Carlson, the commander of the 2nd Raider Battalion, was shipped out. He was assigned to be executive officer of the new 1st Marine Regiment that was being formed, but he fell ill with malaria and jaundice and had to go into the hospital in San Diego. After that he was assigned to Hollywood as technical adviser for the film *Gung Ho,* a heroic motion picture made of his own Raider battalion's exploits. The film was an enormous success and brought great public honor to the Raiders. What the Marine Corps and the navy thought is another matter; the navy generally disliked publicity, although its top commanders were beginning to learn of its value from General MacArthur. Evans Carlson was close to the Roosevelt family, and this made the Marine Corps nervous. He was also a very prickly person, who quarreled with Marine Corps policy. So after Guadalcanal, really, Carlson's career went up on the shelf.

While the 1st and 2nd Marine Raider Battalions were fighting on Guadalcanal, two other battalions were being organized and trained. Lieutenant Colonel Harry Liversedge commanded the new 3rd Raider Battalion on Samoa. Major James Roosevelt was detached from the 2nd Raider Battalion and ordered to form the 4th Raider Battalion and train the men in San Diego.

The 3rd Raider Battalion was the next to be employed. Admiral Halsey decided it would be used to assist in the capture of the Russell Islands, Pavuvu, Banika, Lona, and Alokon, which lie just off Guadalcanal's Cape Esperance.

Although there were no Japanese troops in the Russell Islands, Halsey was concerned lest the enemy make a landing there and threaten Guadalcanal all over again. That was why he decided to capture the Russells first and make them into an American base.

The occupation would be carried out by most of the army 43rd Infantry Division. February 21 was the day set. Five days earlier Lieutenant Murray Ehrlich of the 3rd Raider Battalion and Sergeant Frank Cutting were landed on Banika, the second largest Russell island. One of their objectives was to scout Renard Sound as a possible PT boat base. They moved around the island, established the fact that there were no Japanese present, and then moved across to Pavuvu, the big island. They came back with information for Colonel Liversedge about sites for camps and supply dumps.

The 3rd Raider Battalion landed by rubber boat from destroyer transports on the northern end of Pavuvu Island. They were ashore at seven A.M. The landings were unopposed, and as the Raiders scouted the islands around the edge of the Russells, they found no Japanese. The only danger came from the air; their camp was strafed by Japanese planes, but only once, and on that occasion two of the Japanese planes were shot down. The Raiders were withdrawn from the Russells on March 20, their scouting jobs done.

The 3rd Raiders then went back to Noumea only to discover that big changes were taking place. Lieutenant Colonel Liversedge was promoted to colonel and given command of the new 1st Marine Regiment. This regiment was slated to be a Raider regiment, made up of the four battalions. Lieutenant Colonel Samuel S. Beaton took over the 3rd Raider Battalion. Lieutenant Colonel Alan Shapley succeeded Carlson as commander of the 2nd Raider Battalion. Major Roosevelt came to Noumea with his men of the 4th Raiders, and the regiment was formed.

Halsey had just the place to use the Raider Regiment: New Georgia Island.

New Georgia is just about halfway between Guadalcanal on the south and Rabaul on the north. This big island, forty-five miles long and twenty miles wide, was to be the next stepping stone on the road to Rabaul.

One reason for choosing New Georgia as the next objective was its airfield at Munda Point. This field was about two thirds of the distance from Rabaul to Guadalcanal, and the Japanese used it as a staging base for attacks on Guadalcanal. The Japanese had built their field 4,700 feet long and had been operating it since December. The Japanese had brought in a squadron of planes, but these were almost immediately destroyed by Allied aircraft, and thereafter the Japanese had used Munda Field only for refueling planes from Rabaul.

On March 21 a group of highly trained marine scouts, from the 3rd Raider Battalion and a special scout school built on Guadalcanal, flew into New Georgia aboard a PBY patrol bomber and landed at Segi Plantation on the southwest tip of the island. There they met Donald G. Kennedy, a coastwatcher.

Kennedy had been district officer for Santa Isabel Island, located across the slot from New Georgia. He had moved to Segi Point after the Japanese had invaded the Solomon Islands. There, although completely surrounded by the Japanese, he had survived and set up an early warning system for Henderson Field, 160 miles away. It had helped the Allies immensely in the past six months.

Segi Plantation was isolated, approachable only from the sea since there was no road through the jungle. Kennedy's people had successfully ambushed every party that came along. But not long before this date, at least one Japanese had escaped and had returned to Kolombangara to tell of the coastwatcher. Kennedy was beginning to feel nervous, and he so told the marines as they came in.

He provided them with native guides, and the group split into patrols to go out to look for good landing beaches and possible PT boat bases. The marines traveled by night and observed by day. They looked around Munda, and they scouted the other islands of the group: Rendova, Kolombangara, and Vangunu, all of which housed Japanese military units. Halsey had hoped to land at Segi Plantation and sweep on up to Munda in a simple operation. But the beach at Segi Plantation was too short to handle a major invasion, and the jungle between the plantation and Munda was deep and trackless. So the Raiders went back to Guadalcanal to report and came back to New Georgia with new instructions. All spring long the patrols circulated, bringing back many discouraging reports about the terrain. Finally on June 18 a last patrol came to New Georgia and selected four landing sites: Rendova, Rice Anchorage, Viru Harbor, and Wickham Anchorage. None of them was perfect. All others were impossible. Meanwhile the need for an attack on the New Georgia group became ever more important. The Japanese this spring had concentrated on their attempt to capture all of New Guinea, and were using the New Georgia islands as a staging base. A new airfield was built on Kolombangara Island. In May Major General Noboru Sasaki came to New Georgia to direct the Japanese defense against the attack they were waiting for. The airfields were ringed with antiaircraft guns, and highly trained troops, many of them veterans from China, were sent to the islands. They were waiting. So were the Raiders. And early in June came the word: the invasion of New Georgia was on, and it would be called Operation Toenails. It would be a complex move. The troops had three major objectives:

1. Capture Wickham Anchorage and Viru Harbor for use by small craft.
2. Capture Segi Plantation as a site for an airfield.
3. Seize Rendova Island as a base for the artillery to fire on Munda.

All this was preliminary to the real move: capture of Munda airfield. To undertake this, elements of the 4th Raiders and the 1st Raider Battalion would be employed. The first units to go in were two Raider companies of the 4th Raider Battalion. They were summoned on an emergency basis at the request of coastwatcher Kennedy, who was now being harried by the Japanese. After General Sasaki arrived, he looked over his defenses and suddenly became aware of this coastwatcher, who had been operating so effectively in behalf of the Americans for months. Somebody, General Sasaki learned, was giving the Americans a lot of information about Japanese air operations. Every time they sent down an air attack on Guadalcanal and it stopped in at Munda to refuel, by the time it reached Guadalcanal the Americans were alert and fighters were waiting for the Japanese bombers. The losses were very high, and General Sasaki believed it was because of the intelligence the Allies possessed. The finger pointed straight at someone on New Georgia, and Sasaki believed that someone was Kennedy down on his plantation. On June 17 General Sasaki sent a large force to Viru Harbor to catch Kennedy and his natives.

Within a matter of hours Kennedy had the word, and he got on the radio and cried for help.

Major Masao Hara had been dispatched with a company of special naval landing force troops to take care of Kennedy once and for all. The force headed purposefully toward Segi Plantation. Coastwatcher Kennedy and his natives took to the hills. Then, on June 20 the destroyers *Dent* and *Waters* carried the men of the 4th Raider Battalion to New Georgia. It was a dangerous mission for the destroyers; the water was shallow around Segi Plantation and full of reefs.

A local native pilot came aboard one of the destroyers as they approached Segi and sighted in on bonfires set by Kennedy's men on the beach. Still, the destroyers had plenty of difficulty. There were so many reefs that the island of Vangunu seemed to be a part of New Georgia. The destroyers scraped bottom coming in, but they got in at 5:30 on the morning of June 21, and five hours later the destroyers were on their way out, mission accomplished. The next day two more destroyers delivered two army companies to support the Raiders.

Coastwatcher Kennedy and his radio moved across the channel to Vangunu Island to continue his work of alerting the Allied air forces and navy about the movements of the Japanese, and the Raiders settled down to deal with Major Hara when he showed up.

So the Toenails operations began informally and a little bit prematurely. Soon navy construction battalion troops came in to build an airstrip at Segi, bringing bulldozers and power equipment. They were building an airstrip that was to be ready for use by July 10. The army sent in two companies of infantrymen of the 103rd Infantry. They dug in around the area to defend Segi Plantation, and Lieutenant Colonel Michael S. Currin of the 4th Raider Battalion set out on the offensive to find Major Hara and eliminate his troops. He did not find the major, so he planned an attack on the garrison at Viru. That harbor was protected by a company of Colonel Genjiro Hirata's 229th Regiment, plus a number of artillery troops who had some heavy artillery to protect the harbor.

Major Hara was coming with another infantry company and a machine-gun platoon from the 1st Battalion of the 229th, and he had orders to comb the whole area around Viru until he found the troublesome coastwatcher. And at Viru the defenders had been informed of Kennedy's whereabouts. Lieutenant Harumasa

Adachi was planning an attack very soon on Segi Plantation. But other events intervened.

Admiral Turner soon sent the word: he wanted Viru Harbor in a hurry as a base for PT boats. So Captain Foster LaHue was sent with a guide to look the place over from the Hele Islands in Blanche Channel. He found that the harbor was ideal, with a three-hundred-yard-wide entrance, and a length of eight hundred feet.

Currin was going to attack Regi, a village seven miles from Viru Harbor. From this point he could move his troops overland to a place east of the Viru River and then attack down both sides of the river to seize the village of Tombe on the east bank and Tetemara on the west bank. He was then to strike west and seize the coast guns that were reportedly located at Tetemara. After that, two destroyer transports would sail into Viru Harbor and land a 350-man occupation force.

In order to accomplish this, Colonel Currin would have to ignore the timetable set up by Admiral Turner's planners. After twenty days of scouting in the jungle, Currin knew that he needed more time to get into position than he would have if he did not start moving before the end of June. So he asked permission to begin operations on June 27, and the permission was granted. At nine A.M. on June 27 the marines boarded their rubber boats and started paddling down the river, the eight miles to Regi. Colonel Currin led the way in a big New Georgian war canoe, accompanied by the native guides. Later, one marine told this tale to the official marine historian: It was a weird, moonless night, with black rubber boats on black water, slipping silently through the many islands of Panga Bay. The trip was uneventful except for one scare. It came just before reaching Regi, while lying offshore waiting for word from native scouts who had gone ahead to see if there were any Japanese in the village. While the marines waited nervously, the moon came up rapidly, a half silver moon, which cast a weak reflection. And in that reflection suddenly appeared an object. It looked like a Japanese destroyer! But a moment later the object was identified as a small island. The panic was ended. The scouts came back to report that there were no Japanese in the area, and the men began to land. By one o'clock in the morning of June 28 the Raiders were ashore, and the rubber boats were on their way back to Segi, towed by natives in their war canoes. At dawn the Raiders began their attack.

—15—

New Georgia Jungle

While Colonel Currin was to secure the Viru area, as one part of the New Georgia landings on June 30, another element of the 4th Raider Battalion was to take part in the capture of Vangunu Island. That island was to be made into a supply base to serve between the lower Solomons and the Munda area. The prize was Wickham Anchorage, a sheltered harbor between Vangunu and Gatukai islands.

Besides the Raiders, the task would be carried out by troops of the 103rd Army Infantry and Seabees of the 20th Naval Construction Battalion. Major James E. Clark would lead the two companies of Raiders. They would land at dawn on June 30 at Oloana Bay from destroyer transports and establish a beachhead. The army troops would land half an hour later from LCIs and another contingent would come in by LST. Then the Raiders would move inland, while the army

would move along the beach. Coastwatcher Kennedy
had reported that there were about a hundred Japanese
around this place.

The transports carrying these troops set out for
Purvis Bay on Florida Island and assembled there.
They sailed up north of the Russell Islands toward the
debarkation point at Oloana Bay. They arrived at 2:30
in the morning of June 30. The scouts sent out earlier
had set bonfires on the beaches and were using signal
lights to guide the invading force in, but just then a
heavy tropical storm struck, and in the battering rain
virtually nothing could be seen. The wind was raging.
The seas were heaving, and the destroyer transports
were having enormous difficulty. The landing craft
were put over the sides of the ships, but the marines
found it very hard to get down into them.

And so Admiral George H. Fort, commander of the
invasion, delayed landing until either the weather
cleared or dawn made the beach visible.

The object of Lieutenant Colonel Currin's Raiders
was to reach Viru Harbor and capture the coastal guns
there before the American landing forces came in by
destroyer transport on D-Day, which was June 30. The
colonel was concerned lest they run out of time. And
when they had nearly reached Regi, the reasons for
his concern became obvious. There they ran into a
mangrove swamp two miles wide, an expanse of water,
twisted roots, creepers, and shifting muddy bottom.
There was no way to go around; the marines had to go
through, and so they started to cross.

The Raiders had not gotten very far, when a five-
man Japanese patrol stumbled out of the jungle onto
the rear guard of the Raider column. Company P's 3rd

Platoon killed four of these Japanese after a brief firefight, but one got away. Soon, at around 11:15 that morning, another Japanese patrol stumbled into the rear guard from a side trail. This time the Japanese got between the last five men and the column. Company P riflemen and machine gunners drove the Japanese off, but the five men at the tail end of the line had to disappear in the jungle to avoid the Japanese, and then they lost contact with the column of marines, so they returned to the landing place, found a native canoe, and paddled their way to Segi.

The going for the Raiders was very difficult. That first day they made only six miles, and as they moved inland the terrain grew steadily harder to negotiate. It was a matter of crawling—sometimes on all fours—up one steep mountain and then down the other side into a deep gorge, and then repeating the procedure. The going was even slower than Lieutenant Colonel Currin had expected it would be, and it was apparent to him that he was going to have great difficulty in making his assault on schedule. That night the marines bivouacked almost back-to-back in a very close perimeter, ate their K rations, and huddled beneath their ponchos in the rain that came down all night long.

Colonel Currin sent a native runner back to Segi with a message for Rear Admiral Fort, commander of the force that would land troops at Viru. The Raiders would not be able to make the target date, and needed one more day, he said. But the messengers had their difficulties in getting to Segi, and when they arrived, coastwatcher Kennedy had trouble getting through to navy headquarters in the Russell Islands. The result was that the message arrived too late. Admiral Fort had already sailed and was going to invade on schedule.

On the second day the going for the Raiders got even rougher. They had to cross the Choi River twice; and the Choi River was swift and four times its usual size because of the rains. At two o'clock in the afternoon the Raiders ran into a large Japanese patrol that began firing on them from the right. Captain Anthony Walker, commander of Company P, sent Lieutenant Devillo W. Brown with a reinforced platoon of sixty men to take on the Japanese. They found the enemy dug in on the crest of a hill, about three hundred yards off the trail. They attacked straightaway, and routed the Japanese. On top of the hill they counted eighteen Japanese bodies. But they had lost five marines killed and one wounded. The Raiders buried their dead, made a stretcher for the wounded man, and carried him along. They hurried to catch up with the Currin column. They caught up because the column had to cross the Choi River one more time. After that the exhausted marines stopped for the night and there Lieutenant Brown and his men found the others.

Currin spent most of the night trying to raise Guadalcanal on the radio, but without success. He had no idea whether his runners had gotten through to Segi.

On the morning of June 30 the Raiders moved out again. They were still a full day's march from Viru.

Off Vangunu, the destroyer transports labored in the storm. At 3:45, still out of sight of the land, the destroyer commander decided the ships had been put in the wrong position and moved them a half mile to the east. The landing craft were already going in because the destroyers had not gotten the word from

Admiral Fort that the landing was delayed. Now they became disoriented in relation to their ships. The landing craft were nearly run down by the incoming LCIs bearing the army infantry, and they scattered like water bugs, thus confusing the landings completely. The marines ended up landing all along a seven-mile stretch of the coast, and six boats were lost, but no men were killed or wounded. Two boats of Company Q of the 4th Raiders landed on a reef seven miles west of Oloana Bay. Lieutenant James Brown of the 1st Platoon was riding in one landing craft which lost its rudder on the reef. The marines tied buckets to the boat and used them as sea anchors to guide the boat to shore. The boat carrying Lieutenant Eric S. Holmgrain's 2nd Platoon broached in the surf on the reef and the marines had to swim or wade two miles to shore. They were many hours in getting to Vanganu.

The other marines regrouped at Oloana Bay. They met no opposition as they waited for the army to come in. The soldiers arrived at seven A.M. Then they learned that the Japanese were not at the village of Vura as expected but at another village about a thousand yards northeast of Vura. The troops moved out toward the Kaeruka River, at eight A.M., in a pouring rainstorm. The marines and part of the army force moved inland along a coastwatcher trail unknown to the Japanese, but the trail had been turned into a mudslide, and the marines and soldiers had to drag one another along. They got to the Kaeruka River, and had to ford, using ropes to stay together.

At two o'clock that afternoon of June 30 the attack on the Japanese in the Kaeruka area began. The marines had to cross the river to get at the Japanese, who had many snipers in the trees, and the going was very

difficult from the beginning, all the more so because
the heavy rain had put all the radios out of working
order. Marines and army soldiers got separated, and
the attack came to a halt. But then the center force of
soldiers moved forward and split the Japanese, who
scattered, and the marines pressed on the village of
Kaeruka. When the battle ended, the Japanese had
lost 120 killed, the marines had 12 killed and 21
wounded, and the army had 10 killed and 22 wounded.
That evening Major Clark established a perimeter defense along the beach east of the river.

At two A.M. the Japanese tried to bring three barges
onto the beach, not knowing the Americans had taken
over. This supply run was ambushed, and in a fight
that lasted half an hour most of the Japanese were
killed or escaped by swimming away.

Outside Viru on the morning of June 30, Lieutenant
Colonel Currin's column was to attack Major Hara's
350-man defense force at Viru, to destroy the Japanese
fighting power, and then to wreck installations and
silence the coastal three-inch gun and the other guns.
Three destroyers, the *Hopkins, Crosby,* and *Kilty,*
were carrying in the occupation force of army troops.
But coastwatcher Kennedy had finally gotten through
to Guadalcanal, and Guadalcanal had finally gotten
through to Commander Leith, so he knew he was
sailing into trouble. At 7:30 that morning the ships
came into range of the three-inch shore gun and the
shells began falling around the destroyer transports.
So Commander Leith turned the ships around and
moved back to the mouth of the harbor. There he
steamed back and forth until ten A.M., waiting. He
also got in touch with Admiral Fort for orders, and

they agreed that the destroyers should not brave the coastal guns. Leith landed his men at Nono and they headed overland toward Viru.

At Viru, Major Hara reported triumphantly to General Sasaki at Munda Point that the Hara force had repelled an American invasion.

That morning Colonel Currin's column reached the trail fork where one branch led to Viru and the other south to Tombe. He decided to send a large force down the east side of the inlet to Tombe. Captain Walker was sent down with two platoons from Company P. Colonel Currin headed toward Viru with the rest of the column.

The going toward Viru became harder and harder. The column had to ford the Viru River, and then follow a ridge line along the course of the Tita River, cross the Tita, and climb another mountain. It was dusk when they came out of the jungle on the bank of the Mango River, fifty yards wide, deep, and swift. The marines clasped hands and began to move across, weighted down with guns, machine guns, ammunition, and supplies. By the time they crossed the Mango River, it was dark, and they found themselves stumbling along in a mangrove swamp, waist-deep, their feet catching in the snaky roots under the water. The column stopped. The native guides went to the edges of the swamp and brought back "tree lights," phosphorescent wood from dead logs, and by holding these, the marines were able to maintain contact as they moved along slowly through the swamp. Four hours passed, and finally the marines stumbled out of the swamp. Now they had one half mile to go, up the slope of a mountain at the rear of Tetemara village. The trail was slick and muddy, and as more marines went up it became slicker. They crawled on hands and knees the last one hundred yards to the top and arrived, exhausted.

On the other side of the Viru River, Captain Walker's column had a much easier time of it, and bivouacked that night not far from Tombe. On the morning of July 1 the marines launched their assault on the Japanese at nine o'clock in the morning. They attacked and the Japanese were surprised; thirteen were killed and the rest of the garrison fled. The Raiders did not lose a man.

The firing at Tombe aroused the Japanese across the river at Tetemara, but as they began to move to discover what was happening, they were attacked from the air by marine fighters and bombers. Currin's men, deep in the jungle above Tetemara, could hear the explosions and the machine guns, but they could not see what was happening. It was fifteen minutes before the Currin column broke into the open outside the village and launched their attack. Lieutenant Raymond O. Luckel led the assault with Company O. They moved down the hill and tried to herd the Japanese into an area bordered by the harbor and the sea. But the enemy had established their own main line of defense, and they held it firmly. The marines were stopped. The marines began to inch forward. At the end of an hour they had gained a hundred yards. They moved to the left, and by one o'clock in the afternoon they reached a crest of ground, with Tetemara down the slope. The Japanese then withdrew to the northeast. From the yelling going on along the Japanese line, Currin was sure that the enemy would soon launch a banzai charge, and he reinforced his left flank. Sure enough, the banzai charge came just after two more machine guns and reinforcing riflemen had been sent to the left. The machine guns did the job, the banzai charge was broken, and the marines took Tetemara and the three-inch gun that had driven off the three destroyers earlier. The marines counted the enemy dead—forty-eight of the defenders. They had the three-inch gun, four 80mm guns, eight dual-purpose field and antiaircraft guns, sixteen machine guns, and plenty of ammunition and food. The attack had been very successful, except that eight marines had been killed in the fighting.

That afternoon Currin's men saw that they had come just in time. Three LCTs sailed into the harbor, carrying fuel and ammunition for the occupation forces. Just then the occupying force was the 4th Raider Battalion's men, for the 103rd Infantrymen were struggling through the jungle toward Viru, and would not arrive for three days. The Raiders stayed until the infantrymen had regained their strength, but on July 10 the Raiders set out for Guadalcanal. They had accomplished their difficult mission, had prepared the way for the new base at Viru Harbor, and had lost thirteen men killed and fifteen injured of a force of 375 officers and men.

Major Hara had been under orders before the destroyers arrived off Viru to abandon his defenses and hurry to Munda to assist in the defense of the airfield area. He fought the battle of Tetemara in spite of those orders, and lost many of his men and much of his material, and then marched to Munda. The going was just as hard for the Japanese as it had been for the Americans, and it took them about two weeks to make it to Munda. Stragglers came in for days, for the original Hara force of about 350 men had been all cut up. Sixty-one Japanese had been killed and a hundred wounded. Some of the wounded made it back to Munda, but slowly. Hara brought about 170 men back in a column to participate in the defense of Munda.

On Vangunu on the morning of July 1, patrols discovered that the Japanese remnants were digging in at Cheke Point, about five hundred yards east of the Kaeruka River. The American overall commander was Colonel Brown of the army, and he chose not to attack the Japanese but to set up defenses at Vura village. The Japanese were then attacked from the air by American marine aircraft and from the sea by Admiral Fort's destroyers, until they evacuated the Cheke Point area, with the loss of eight men killed.

On July 4 the Raiders were detached from Colonel Brown's forces and sent back to Oloana Bay aboard LCIs. Then they were ordered to Gatukai Island, east of Vangunu, to look for some fifty Japanese who were reported to be there. They patrolled the island for two days but did not find any Japanese. They went back to Oloana Bay, and on July 12 returned to Guadalcanal to rejoin Colonel Currin and the rest of the 4th Marine Raider Battalion.

—16—

The Siege of New Georgia

General Sasaki at Munda and General Imamura at Rabaul were not quite sure what was going on in the southern Solomons. Monitoring the Allied radio traffic and learning that the flow of messages was very heavy in the middle of June, they fully expected a major invasion. But the invasion of Segi on June 21 and the march on Viru a few days later was accompanied by a fall in radio traffic. The reason was that all the necessary messages pertaining to the New Georgia invasion had been sent. But this change persuaded the Japanese that they had been wrong, and that the Segi and Viru actions were nothing more than raids like that on Makin Island in the Gilberts.

For that reason the Japanese changed their defense plans. Admiral Kusaka, the commander of the Japanese Southeast Area fleet, had sent the main elements of the 11th Air Fleet from Rabaul down to Buin in order to oppose the New Georgia landings. But when no landings came by June 25, Kusaka decided he had been wrong and brought the air fleet back up to Rabaul.

Admiral Turner's main invasion fleet was at sea on June 29, six transports and two destroyer transports, protected by several destroyers, headed for Rendova, the island that lies south of New Georgia's Munda Point. They sailed from Koli Point on Guadalcanal, north of the Russell Islands, and then turned west and northwest to head up Blanche Channel. To confuse the Japanese, ships were sent to Buin and Vila to bombard Japanese installations just as the ships of the invasion force dropped anchor in Rendova Bay. Even when the Japanese discovered this, they did not understand what the Allies were doing. The answer was really quite simple. The Allies were landing on Rendova to install heavy artillery there, and thus the invasion of Munda would be protected.

The Japanese wondered what in the world the Americans wanted with Rendova. They had no important installations there and only a few garrison troops. Most of these were stationed at the old Lever Brothers plantation. The island is eight miles wide and twenty miles long, but most of it is densely jungled mountain or swamp. The best anchorage was Rendova Harbor, a cove a mile and a half long and three quarters of a mile wide, which had two deep water entrances behind three small islands.

The eight screening destroyers stood offshore while the transports and destroyer transports unloaded their troops, beginning at 6:40 on the morning of June 30.

But as the landing craft swooped into the entrance to the harbor and plowed into the shore, they were greeted by a hail of machine-gun and small-arms fire. That was not supposed to happen. The plan had called for scout troops of the 172nd Army Infantry to land an hour earlier and secure the beach. But the troops' landing craft had gotten lost in the heavy storm that covered the whole area, and the leaders had missed the signal fires set by the natives for them, and they had drifted down the island ten miles before landing. By the time they arrived on the scene, the landings were already in full gear.

The whole landing operation was sloppy. The first troops had moved up only about fifteen yards, which gave no room for landing of supplies and equipment. The landing craft kept shuttling back and forth from ship to shore, bringing more, more, more, and soon the beach was a mass of equipment and vehicles, all crowded together. From the plantation Japanese machine gunners occasionally fired a few bursts toward the beach, which added to the confusion. No one was ashore to organize the infantry into patrols or to lead them against the enemy, so they stayed put. Snipers in the trees harried the beachhead and no one went after them. It was several hours before the offensive got going, and by that time most of the Japanese at the Lever plantation had fled into the hills.

One thing was clear: The army and the navy still had a lot to learn about amphibious invasions.

The Japanese defense effort was also substandard. The heavy rain had wetted the Japanese garrison's radios and they would not work. Across the channel, General Sasaki knew nothing of the invasion for several hours, because the whole area was shrouded in storm clouds and heavy rain. Finally a signal was sent by light, which Sasaki received. Then his artillery began to fire on the Rendova beachhead, but it was aimless fire because visibility was so poor. Only the destroyer *Gwin* was hit. Since the air force had moved back to Rabaul, there was no air attack. Three hours after the invasion, the area was more or less clear of Japanese, with about sixty-five dead Japanese lying around the plantation area.

The beach was still confused, the effect of a serious tactical miscalculation. The trouble was that no beach organization had been set up and no working party had been provided. So infantrymen were pressed into service to move supplies and the barracks bags that were piling up on the beach. Trucks came off the ships and were loaded, and moved up to the plantation area. But after a half dozen trucks had sloshed up the trail, the roadbed had become a quagmire, and trucks began bogging down in the sticky mud. Tractors had to be brought up to pull them free. Finally the mud became so deep that only the amphibious tractors of the 9th Marine Defense Battalion and the bulldozers of the Seabees could move at all. At first the lighters could not get in to shore, and troops had to wade out fifty feet in knee-deep water to carry the supplies in. Later the Seabees dug coral with their bulldozers and made coral ramps out to the lighter area. Finally the whole unloading process had to be stopped because the vehicles were bogged down, and much of the supply had to be diverted to other islands. By mid-afternoon Admiral Turner decided to take his ships back to Guadalcanal, expecting air attack. He had scarcely begun the voyage when the attack came, about fifty Japanese planes coming in over Munda Point. The admiral's flagship, the *McCawley,* was torpedoed, then bombed, and had to be abandoned. That night she was sunk by three torpedoes fired by an American PT boat whose crew thought they were shooting at a Japanese destroyer. During the next few days the troops ashore on Rendova took a beating from Japanese bombers but the landings on New Georgia began at Zanana Beach. They were supposed to be preceded by a company of the 4th Raider Battalion, but these troops were still at Segi and Viru.

The Raiders did get into action on New Georgia, however. Colonel Liversedge's Northern Landing Group came ashore at Rice Anchorage on the northern shore of New Georgia as the army troops were marching toward their line of departure along the Barike River. From there they were to go inland to attack Munda airfield. Colonel Liversedge was to threaten Munda from the north.

Almost immediately the army troops on the Barike River met determined Japanese resistance and bogged down. The 172nd Regiment moved a little. The 169th went into bivouac when it hit opposition. Ten days after the beginning of the invasion, the commander and staff of the 169th were relieved and replaced. A few days later the American ground force commander was superseded in an effort to get this offensive moving.

The original plans for the New Georgia operation had called for Colonel Liversedge's 1st Marine Raider Regiment to be used as a reserve. But two battalions had already been committed to other efforts before the invasion began.

And then the intelligence officers learned of the existence of a Japanese garrison of about five hundred troops plus some coastal defense guns at Bairoko harbor across the island from Munda. What worried the intelligence men was the road that ran from Bairoko and the Munda airfield. On this road Vila was the main source of Japanese reinforcement and supply. Also, Bairoko was the central point in the complex Japanese barge supply system, which served the whole New Georgia chain of islands. So it was decided to send Colonel Liversedge to take Bairoko to cut off the flow to General Sasaki.

Liversedge's orders called for him to take the remainder of his Raider regiment, plus the 2nd Battalion of the 148th Army Infantry and land at Rice Anchorage, a narrow beach on the Pundakona River. After the landing the troops were to move southwest, clearing out the Japanese in the Bairoko and Enogai Inlet region. They were also—and this was very important—to establish roadblocks across all trails and roads leading from Bairoko to Munda. All that done, Liversedge was to send men along the trail from Bairoko to Munda as far as possible, to prevent reinforcement of General Sasaki.

The whole area around Enogai and Bairoko was virtually unknown territory. It was called the Dragons Peninsula; there were no good aerial maps, and the natives of Guadalcanal and the Segi Point area were reluctant to go there because of the animosity of the local tribesmen.

Because so little was known about this region, and because the 4th Raider Battalion was still tied down at Viru, Colonel Liversedge was given another battalion, the 3rd Battalion of the 145th Infantry. The invasion date was set for July 5, 1943.

The troops prepared. They would take in only their

infantry weapons and light machine guns, 60mm mortars and 81mm mortars, and the heavy machine guns of the army battalions. They had no field artillery but would have to rely on air strikes if they needed that sort of support.

Shortly after midnight on July 5 the bombardment of the Bairoko area began from a cruiser-destroyer force accompanying the invasion troops. Immediately the marines got a surprise: from the Enogai area the ships were fired on by field pieces. No one had reported any field pieces in this area, and so the surprise was considerable. The destroyers and cruisers shifted their fire to Enogai and tried to silence the guns. The Japanese navy took a hand that night, too, and a Japanese destroyer torpedoed the American destroyer *Strong,* which sank almost immediately.

Colonel Liversedge began landing his troops at 1:30 in the morning. It was raining again, a torrential downpour that made it almost impossible to see the shore from the sea, except by the light of the shellfire. They could not even find Rice Anchorage in the murk. The whole column of ships stopped, the captains very nervous about those Japanese destroyers lurking in the area, and one destroyer with a radar sweep went ahead to try to find the anchorage. The destroyer located the mouth of the Pundakona River. After that, confidence returned. The troops got ready to go ashore, and marines and soldiers climbed down into the landing craft. Enemy shelling began, and starshells lit up the attack force and splashed down among the transports.

The landing craft were delayed when they ran up against a shallow sandbar that blocked the entrance to Rice Anchorage. Some of the supplies had to be offloaded before the landing craft could get across, towing the marines and soldiers in ten-man rafts. When they did get to the beach they found it was a narrow shelf hacked out of the jungle, and only four boats at a time could beach to unload. Luckily there were no Japanese in the area.

Soon soldiers and marines were sliding around on the muddy beach, tripping over banyan roots and cursing the darkness. The Japanese were firing from Bairoko and Enogai, but they obviously were not aware of the exact location of the anchorage, since their fire went well overhead and off into the jungle. Just before dawn everything was landed that could be, and Colonel Liversedge gave the word to the ships offshore. "Scram," he said, and they scrammed with alacrity. Counting noses, Colonel Liversedge realized that one company of the army infantry was missing. Those men had gone astray and landed farther north along the coast. It took them a half day to find their way to the anchorage.

Waiting for Liversedge and his men were Flight Lieutenant J. A. Corrigan, an Australian coast-watcher, and Captain Clay A. Boyd of the 1st Marine Raider Regiment and a force of about two hundred New Georgian natives, who had agreed to help the Allies in this campaign. Boyd had scouted much of this area in the past few weeks, including a trail that led from Rice Anchorage to Enogai. The New Georgians had then chopped parallel trails on both sides of this trail. So when the Northern Landing Group (as it was called) landed, the natives and the soldiers and marines bundled up the supplies and set forth toward Enogai on the three trails. Company A and Company

B of the Raider Regiment's 1st Raider Battalion moved along the left-hand trail, led by Lieutenant Colonel Griffith. The demolitions platoon took the trail on the right. The main elements of the landing force took the middle trail, with the marines leading and the army men following. Two army companies and a medical detachment remained behind to guard the supply dump.

Liversedge's 1st Marine Raider Regiment was about to go into action for the first time.

—17—

Enogai

The advance scouts had it all wrong about the terrain of that part of New Guinea. They said Enogai was remarkable for its open jungle with small broken hills and few swamps. But the Raiders and their army friends found no such terrain. They slogged through the rain and treacherously slippery mud, up steep inclines made even worse by banyan roots that were slicked with green moss and interspersed near the shore with outcroppings of coral. The "open jungle" turned out to be a mass of brush and creepers that tore at their clothes and hindered the movement of heavy equipment.

The army soldiers were much the worse off. Their equipment had not been designed for this sort of travel. The heavy machine guns, the mortar base plates, the .50-caliber ammunition, all bogged the soldiers down. They could not keep up with the more lightly laden Raiders, and they dragged behind. Sometimes they stopped altogether and cached some of the heavy equipment in dumps. The leading marine groups heading south (along a very tortuous route) reached the Giza Giza River late in the afternoon. There they stopped and set up a perimeter defense for the night. They had traveled five miles, although they believed they had traveled eight miles. By dark the army units had caught up and the Americans were camped on both sides of the Giza Giza River.

That night the Raiders heard naval gunfire. They were listening to the battle of Kula Gulf, in which an American force of cruisers and destroyers encountered a Japanese force of ten destroyers that was bringing reinforcements up to General Sasaki. The Japanese lost two destroyers but managed to land nearly a thousand reinforcements. The Americans lost the cruiser *Helena*.

Next morning, still in the pouring rain, the Raiders and the army men moved forward again toward Enogai. The Raiders divided into two units here. Lieutenant Colonel Delbert E. Schultz took the 3rd Battalion of the 148th Infantry along a trail to the southwest where the Munda-Bairoko road lay, and established a roadblock.

From the Giza Giza River the going was much more difficult. The three trails slashed by the New Georgians ended there, and the Americans had to make their own trail between the Giza Giza and the Tamakan rivers. That meant cutting their way through with machetes. They were in mangrove swamp again, slipping and sliding through the rain. The army men laid wire for field telephones, but the rubber cover of the wire peeled away in the hands of the men, who were using it to guide them, and the lines grounded and were useless. The Raiders' radios also failed as the water drowned the batteries. Colonel Liversedge kept in touch with the base at Rice Anchorage in the age-old way, using native runners with messages.

Captain Boyd and Raider Company D reached the Tamakan River shortly before noon. It was supposed to be a small stream, easily fordable. Or that was how it had been four weeks earlier, when Boyd had scouted it. But now the rains had swollen the river to create a torrent. The Raiders had to ferry equipment across on rafts made of branches and their ponchos. Then the infantrymen began to cross on a fallen tree which bridged the stream. A rope was stretched to help, and strong swimmers stood by to save those who fell in. It was slow going and the crossing was not completed until late that afternoon. It was still raining. Colonel Liversedge ordered a bivouac that night of July 6 in the middle of the banyan swamp. Tired Raiders and soldiers dropped where they were, ate cold rations out of cans, and huddled against the rain in their ponchos.

Late that night Colonel Liversedge was in touch by radio with General Hester, the commander of the Munda landing force. Nothing was learned. At dawn the men began to move again. It was still raining.

The marines and soldiers moved along the swamp and then the swamp ended and they clambered up a ridge line and followed its up and down curves toward the west bank of Enogai Inlet. They heard the sounds of an air strike, and Colonel Liversedge knew it was a strike preordered, which was supposed to be supporting his attack on Enogai. But he was behind schedule so the strike was not meaningful.

Not long before noon the column suddenly ran across seven Japanese soldiers. A firefight began. Two Japanese were killed, but the rest fled. A check of the bodies showed that the Japanese were members of the Special Naval Landing Forces from the Kure 6th Regiment at Enogai.

Colonel Liversedge now realized that his presence would be known to the Enogai garrison. Colonel Griffith was hurried along toward Enogai to see if he could still surprise the Japanese.

The demolitions platoon had the next encounter with the Japanese. They withdrew to high ground and took on the enemy. Captain Boyd's Company D outflanked the Japanese and killed ten of them before the Japanese fled. Three Raiders had been killed and four wounded. They moved on, and by nightfall Griffith's Raiders had occupied the native village of Triri on Enogai Inlet, and Colonel Liversedge was set up at Maranusa.

At Triri the Americans found a Japanese map that showed the location of four 140mm guns at Enogai. The map was rushed to Colonel Liversedge, who got on the radio and ordered an air strike. But his message did not get through. It was, however, picked up by an army station at Viru, which rebroadcast the message toward the Commander of Air, New Georgia.

Early on the morning of July 8, Lieutenant Colonel Griffith was moving forward with two platoons down two tracks north and west from Triri. The idea was to ambush any Japanese before they could make an attack. The marines on the west trail hit first: they ran across a Japanese patrol of company strength, which was moving along the trail without any security. The marines paused to set a trap, but somebody fired his weapon. The Japanese got clean away. Fifteen minutes later the marines were under attack from the Japanese in even greater strength than they had thought. Griffith sent Boyd's Company D down to help out. This was the biggest fight yet. It lasted for three hours. Captain John P. Salmon's Company C came up with 160mm mortars and started a barrage against the Japanese. This forced the enemy to move back. They disengaged, and moved back toward Munda, leaving fifty dead. The marines did not pursue. They had their orders: take Enogai. So they resumed the march along the north trail. But the trail ended in a swamp which was impassable, the marines found. It took hours to discover that there was no way through. They had to go back to Triri and wait until the following day to make a new start in a different direction.

After the Japanese got the word that the Raiders were moving against Enogai, they organized for attack. The shadows were lengthening on the afternoon of July 8 when about four hundred Japanese troops struck the left flank of the perimeter established by the army companies. They began to break through the line of Company K of the 145th Infantry. The demolition platoon of the Raiders rushed up to help the soldiers. Just then Lieutenant Colonel Griffith's battalion returned from its fruitless mission. Colonel Liversedge called on them to help, and Colonel Griffith sent Lieutenant Robert Kennedy's platoon from Company B to encircle the Japanese and hit the left flank. They did so. The surprise attack routed the Japanese and they retreated, leaving twenty dead. Company K estimated that they had also lost another seventy-five men; the army company had three men wounded.

After another night at Triri the Raiders set out again on the morning of July 9 for Enogai. Colonel Liversedge came along with Griffith's battalion. They found a good trail and began to make steady progress toward Enogai. They heard the sounds of an air strike, which was again in support of their activity. Just before noon they caught sight of Leland Lagoon and turned east toward Enogai Point. They continued as the afternoon wore away. Late in the afternoon they came up against machine-gun fire, and as they probed, the firing increased in volume. They had hit the main line of defense of the Japanese at Enogai.

The mortars were back in the column, and so Colonel Liversedge decided to attack without mortar preparation. It was a mistake. The marines struck with machine-gun and grenade support, but the Japanese beat off the attack. It was growing very late, twilight was coming fast, and Liversedge called off the assault. The Raiders were told to hold in place and start again the next morning. They settled down in defensive positions. There was no food left. The Raiders had set out with a three-day food supply, which they had stretched to five days. They were supposed to have a food drop from the air, but it had not come before they attacked on July 10. They had no water either, but this was not a great problem. The Raiders could catch drinking water from the rain in their ponchos.

The Japanese did not make a night banzai attack. But in the middle of the night a huge banyan tree fell to the ground, crushing one Raider and hurting three others, and smashing the command radio to bits.

July 10. Morning. The hungry Raiders were awake, waiting for orders. Colonel Griffith told them to start the attack. Company B, on the right, moved forward. But Company A and Company C ran into a hail of Japanese fire. The mortars came up and began firing. Company B hurried through a small village on the south shore of Enogai. This action put them at the rear of the Japanese, and the pressure on the other two companies stopped. All three companies moved up to Enogai. The mortars took the high ground overlooking the village and began dropping shells along the shore of Kula Gulf. Japanese stragglers, trying to swim across Leland Lagoon, were machine-gunned. By early afternoon only two pockets of Japanese resistance remained at Enogai. These pockets were surrounded and left until the next day. As dusk fell, soldiers of the 145th came into camp, bringing extra ammunition, food, and water. That night the marines ate K rations and Japanese fish, rice, and sake. Their defense perimeter ran from Leland Lagoon to Enogai Inlet, facing toward Bairoko.

That night of July 10 the Japanese evacuated their wounded by barge and picked up stragglers. On the morning of July 11 the marines moved in to clear up the two pockets of resistance. By lunchtime they had the whole area under control. They had lost 47 men killed, 4 men missing, but the Japanese casualties were put at 350. The Raiders had captured the four 140mm guns and many other machine guns and small arms.

Using an army radio, Colonel Liversedge called for PBYs to come and evacuate the wounded, who were now housed in the village huts of Enogai. But a Japanese bombing raid came first on the eleventh, and left three more men dead and fifteen more wounded. When the PBYs picked up the wounded, they were attacked by a pair of Japanese float planes. The marines fired all their weapons at the planes, and the PBYs took off. The fight for Enogai was over. That night seven landing craft from Rice Anchorage came into the inlet with supplies.

—18—

Assault on Bairoko

One of the reasons for sending the 1st Marine Raider Regiment and its attached army units into the Dragons Peninsula had been to stop Japanese reinforcement of the Munda area from Bairoko. To this end, Lieutenant Colonel Schultz's 3rd Battalion of the 148th Army Infantry was sent down a trail that was supposed to join the main Munda-Bairoko trail. At the junction the soldiers were to establish and hold a roadblock.

When the troops moved out, a New Guinea native guide looked at the map they were using and said that the map was all wrong. The trail did not meet the main trail at this point at all. But the New Guinea guides and the Americans had the most fragmentary of communications, by sign language and pidgin, and so the guide was unable to show the soldiers what they should do and where they should go. Consequently the troops marched to a junction of two trails and there set up their roadblock. It seemed right; they found footprints left by many many sets of rubber-soled Japanese shoes.

If he needed proof that he was in the right place, he had it soon enough. Six hours after the roadblock was established, a squad of Japanese approached from Bairoko and were fired on by the troops. They retreated, but two hours later a much larger Japanese force attacked and tried to batter down the American defenses. They failed, and withdrew. The night, July 8, was quiet, and the next morning Colonel Schultz sent patrols down toward Munda, trying to contact the 169th Infantry, which was supposed to be coming this way in its attack on Munda. He did not make contact, but he did find an abandoned Japanese bivouac site, which was more convincing evidence that they were on the right track.

On the morning of July 10 the roadblock was attacked on both flanks by strong forces of Japanese, estimated at fifty to eighty men. This was followed by another attack by an estimated two companies, about four hundred men. The fierce fighting for this position was proof to Colonel Schultz that the roadblock was indeed in the right place.

But the fact was that though the soldiers of the 148th Infantry fought valiantly and kept the Japanese from overrunning their roadblock, they were in the wrong place, and the only real benefit of their roadblock was to kill a certain number, about 150, of Japanese. They should have been at least a half mile closer to Munda, where the main Bairoko-Munda trail lay. As it was, the roadblock did not stop the Japanese from reinforcing Munda by trail as the Americans thought.

The Japanese were also reinforcing the whole area

by sea. On the night of July 12 they sent down another group of transports and destroyers and one light cruiser. The Americans were in Kula Gulf for this second battle, with cruisers and destroyers. The two forces fought, the Americans sank the Japanese cruiser, but lost the destroyer *Gwin* and saw the cruisers *Honolulu, St. Louis,* and the New Zealand cruiser *Leander* damaged. The Japanese put another 1,250 troops ashore, this time on the island of Kolobangara, from which they would make their way by barge to Munda. The success of this landing was a matter of concern to everyone from Admiral Halsey down to Colonel Liversedge because it meant the Japanese might launch a counterlanding in the Enogai-Bairoko area, to wipe out the Liversedge force. With this in mind the marines had strengthened the defenses left by the Japanese, strung barbed wire from Enogai Point across the point to Leland Lagoon, and dug in behind that.

But the Japanese had found the price of this sort of reinforcement too high in ships, and after this second Kula Gulf encounter, they abandoned the idea of using destroyers and transports to resupply Munda, and began using the barge system instead. So although he did not know it, Colonel Liversedge had no cause for worry about a landing.

Colonel Liversedge now established his command post at Enogai. His first move was to check the road-block supposedly on the Bairoko-Munda trail. It was puzzling that after that first fight there had been no more activity along that trail. The colonel took a patrol over there, and after a few hours was convinced that the block was somehow wrong and ought to be abandoned. So on the morning of July 17, Lieutenant

Colonel Schultz abandoned the roadblock and the soldiers went back to Triri, where they had a decent meal and clean clothes for the first time in two weeks.

At Enogai the marines were preparing to move against Bairoko. For two weeks they had been sending patrols down the road and encountering the Japanese, who were doing the same thing. A few fights occurred, but they were almost always broken off with a minimum of casualties. What the patrols did establish was that the Japanese were sturdily ensconced in Bairoko harbor and that they intended to stay there. Some of the patrols had come close enough to see Japanese soldiers digging entrenchments east of the harbor. One patrol also reported having found two good trails leading to high ground east of the Japanese camp that had not been occupied, and that a battalion could reach this point in two and a half hours. That was very tempting information. But the problem was that Colonel Liversedge did not have any information at all about the size of the Japanese defense force.

Because of this, Colonel Liversedge sent a messenger to Guadalcanal to see Admiral Turner and ask for reinforcement. On July 18 he got it; four destroyer transports arrived, and Lieutenant Colonel Currin's 4th Marine Raider Battalion came ashore. But Colonel Liversedge was disappointed to learn that the battalion was two hundred men under strength. The capture of Viru and Vangunu had been costly to the 4th Raider Battalion. Many men had come down sick with malaria after that campaign and they were out of it for the moment. But Colonel Liversedge had asked for reinforcements, and when they were sent he was bound to carry out the expected attack on Bairoko. He still had no clear idea of the extent or strength of the Japanese defenses.

The Raiders and their attached army units were to move on Bairoko in two columns. Company B and Company D of the 1st Raider Battalion and the four companies of the 4th Raider Battalion were to move straight toward Bairoko to attack the northern defenses. This meant taking a route along the south shore of Leland Lagoon.

Lieutenant Colonel Schultz's troops were to move from Triri to hit the south side of the Japanese position. Air strikes were asked on July 19, the day before the attack, and on July 20, which was D-Day. The air attack for the nineteenth was assigned, but that for the twentieth was not. The Solomons air command apparently had better use for its planes that day.

On July 19 the Raiders made a last-minute reconnaissance of the sandspit that led down to Bairoko, and the units that would lead the assault got into position. That afternoon they watched bombers bomb and strafe Bairoko, for the fourth time in recent days. But the marines did not know what the bombers were hitting; they still had no real idea of the size of the Japanese garrison, and higher headquarters had estimated that it was about two reinforced companies. The fact was, however, that the Japanese had the equivalent of two battalions to defend that place, or about fifteen hundred men. And fifteen hundred men was just about what the Raiders and the army force numbered as they set out through the jungle, scrambling over coral and cutting themselves, and moving along the hills and ridges.

The Raiders were to start the attack at 7:30, and the air strike was supposed to come at nine o'clock. But of course no air strike came at all that morning, much to the surprise of Colonel Liversedge and the dismay of his line officers. Without air support, the marines and the army men were in trouble, because they had no artillery and had been told that they did not need it because the air power would provide the same effect.

The column of marines reached the first Japanese outposts at 10:15 and came immediately under fire. The marines overran the outpost and pushed on. By 10:40 they came up against machine-gun fire, which meant they had hit the Japanese line of resistance. Colonel Griffith informed Colonel Liversedge, and the marines pressed on. But here the Japanese were ready. They unleashed a hail of heavy fire. The marines were pinned down by this barrage, but they began firing back.

What they faced was a series of log and coral bunkers dug in under the banyans and camouflaged with palm fronds and branches. The Japanese had built these bunkers so that their guns had interlocking fields of fire. And up in the trees were snipers, some of them with .25-caliber Nambu light machine guns.

The marines in the center and on the right were pinned down, but Company D of the 1st Raider Battalion, now commanded by Lieutenant Frank A. Kemp (Captain Boyd had been evacuated with malaria) began to move on the left, but casualties were high. Colonel Griffith now committed his reserves, the demolition company under Gunner Angus R. Goss, and the Japanese line seemed to give way. Twenty minutes later the advance was continuing. It was very slow going. The technique was to knock out the pillboxes or bunkers. But the means were slight. In later campaigns the marines would have flamethrowers and tanks. Now they had machine guns, rifles, grenades, and 60mm mortars that could not be used because the bunkers were protected by dense jungle. So it was a matter of keeping the bunker under fire while some marine edged up with grenades or explosive charges and tossed them into the bunker.

This way, one bunker after the other was overrun, but at heavy cost.

Just after noon, Colonel Liversedge committed his very last reserve, Colonel Currin's battalion, to the fight for Bairoko. Company P of the battalion moved up but was soon stopped by murderous crossfire from the right and left. The Japanese had done a superb job of planning and building their defenses. The Raiders were gaining, but their gains could be measured in feet. Company B of the 1st Raider Battalion, under Lieutenant William J. Christie, faced a swamp backed by strong bunkers. Seven Japanese machine guns kept the marines from advancing here.

For the next two hours the marines advanced by the foot. They moved through two defense lines. Company D, which was taking heavy casualties, managed to make the top of a ridge overlooking Bairoko harbor five hundred yards away. But between the Raiders and the harbor was another series of fortifications.

By 2:45 P.M. the line now formed a wide U with the center pointed toward the harbor. Then the Japanese opened up with a new weapon, a mortar barrage, which was followed by a counterattack. Kemp's Company D was pinned down, and then hit by the banzai charge. But Kemp organized a counterattack, and surprised the Japanese, sending them reeling back. He then sent a message to Colonel Liversedge, asking for just one more company to help him. If he got that company, they could take the port of Bairoko by nightfall.

But Colonel Liversedge did not have a company to give him. All the reserves had been committed to the fight. Company Q, the only one that had not been engaged in heavy fighting, moved up to the rear of the other 4th Raider Battalion units.

By four P.M. the Japanese had been pushed back into the Bairoko harbor area into a space about three hundred yards wide and eight hundred yards long. Colonel Liversedge ordered Company Q into the line and it began to move, but straight into the face of heavy enemy fire. The attack failed. The Japanese machine guns were just too much. Company Q took very heavy casualties and was forced back, and after that one brief charge was so depleted that it was ineffective as a combat unit.

Thus was the high and low point of the Bairoko attack reached that afternoon. So near, but yet so far. Just one more company of fighting men, at the key moment, and the Japanese could have been pushed back into the sea. But the army units, which were supposed to be coming up, did not make it in time. They bogged down and stopped, planning to attack the next morning. The delay was fatal.

Darkness approached, with the Japanese compressed into their corner of the defenses, and the marines hanging onto the ridges above, but no longer strong enough to make an advance. Colonel Liversedge asked Colonel Griffith to make an appraisal of the situation, and Griffith did. His recommendation was that the marines withdraw. He said, "By this time the Raiders had nearly two hundred fifty casualties, or about thirty percent of the force. We had another one hundred fifty men tied up in getting them evacuated to aid stations and to Enogai. There was nothing to do but to pull back, to reorganize, re-equip, get some rest, try to get something to cope with the Japanese ninety-millimeter mortars, and get the wounded out.

"The decision to pull back was made by Harry the Horse [Liversedge] on recommendation from me after I had talked to Currin and his and my company commanders and had made a personal reconnaissance of the front. Harry had a mission and was understandably loath to abandon it. The final determination was the Japanese capability to reinforce from Vila Stanmore during the night by barge. We were up against a stone wall, low on ammunition, and out of water, and had a responsibility to two hundred wounded men. In any case, reorganization was a paramount requirement."

So near, so far. From the ridge line Colonel Griffith could look down on the harbor, only three hundred yards away. But there was no way they could reach it without more men, more ammunition. Reluctantly Colonel Liversedge gave the order, and just after five P.M. the withdrawal began. The seriously wounded went first, about ninety men carried on litters made of ponchos and tree branches. Then came the walking wounded. And then came the tired, fighting men who had not been hurt, coming slowly, turning to fire on the enemy, and picking up weapons which had been dropped on the way.

Darkness closed down suddenly, and the remainder of the marines retired under its cover. A defense perimeter was set up back on the lagoon. Colonel Liversedge asked for air support again, and then settled down to wait. The Japanese staged one banzai attack, it failed, and there were no more. The Japanese were also exhausted by the effort of that day. Next morning the long, unhappy American march back to Enogai resumed. There the Raiders stayed, ordered to keep their positions and prevent the Japanese from attacking. The campaign was over. It had ended in stalemate.

—19—

Bougainville

Bougainville was the next logical step, for after New Georgia the Allies had decided on a change in policy; they would not make the stair-step approach to Rabaul that had been planned in the beginning. They would not battle for Kolombangara Island, heavily fortified by the Japanese, or all the other Solomon Islands up the chain, but they would strike farther north, at Bougainville, bypassing many garrisons and letting them wither on the vine, so to speak, and they would isolate Rabaul and make its bases unimportant to the future effort. This plan was actually created by the Joint Chiefs of Staff in Washington, although it has often been credited to General MacArthur. But MacArthur certainly saw the intelligence of the plan and gave it his wholehearted endorsement.

Once the decision to land on Bougainville was made, then the question of where on Bougainville to land became vital. Halsey sent several patrols of scouts to figure out the answer. The problem, as everywhere in the Solomons, was that the Allies had only the most sketchy knowledge of the terrain involved. This came from former residents of the islands, mostly planters and missionaries, with a scattering of sea captains and government officials. After much discussion, the two possible landing areas were limited to Empress Augusta Bay and the Kieta area. A navy-marine team with an Australian and four Solomon Islander guides remained in the Kieta area for four days exploring the northeast coast of the island by night, and lying offshore aboard the submarine *Gato* in the daytime. The patrol had some narrow escapes with the many Japanese in this part of the island but returned safely to Guadalcanal on September 28, 1943. Their report on the Kieta area was generally unfavorable: too many shallows and reefs for landings and no suitable site for an airfield.

Another patrol boarded the submarine *Guardfish* and was taken to the Laruma River area of Empress Augusta Bay. They found Cape Torokina, which had a narrow beach, but one that was nearly six miles long, with a suitable site for an airfield. Another plus was the paucity of Japanese in this area; the patrol sighted one lonely sentry and a half dozen Japanese aircraft, and that was all.

That patrol provided the clincher. The marines picked up soil samples, which proved that the coconut grove was indeed suitable as a site for at least a fighter strip. Admiral Halsey was very favorably impressed by the thought of landing in an area where there were virtually no defenders. It would give the men on the beachhead a little time to get set before they faced the expected furious Japanese counterattack. Halsey's opinions were shared by the members of General Alexander Vandegrift's 1st Marine Amphibious Command (IMAC). And so the invasion of Bougainville at Empress Augusta Bay, and specifically at Cape Torokina, was on. On October 1, 1943, Admiral Halsey told General MacArthur that this was it. D-Day was set for November 1.

Halsey never had any idea of capturing all of Bougainville. The island was too big for that, and there were too many Japanese on the island, most of them in the south and extreme north. The best intelligence estimates put the number of Japanese on Bougainville at forty-five thousand troops. These were members of the Imperial Japanese 16th Army under Lieutenant General Haruyoshi Hyukatake, who had commanded the Japanese troops on Guadalcanal and had been largely responsible for the extremely successful evacuation of his sick troops under the noses of the Allies at the end of 1942. The choice of the Empress Augusta Bay area was made, also, because the Cape Torokina plain could be defended by about two divisions of American troops. The defensive area was a rough rectangle about six miles deep and eight miles long between the Laruna River on the north, the mountains on the southwest, the Torokina River on the south, and the sea on the east. It would take about three months for the Japanese in the south to move overland up to this point. The reinforcements then would have to come from the sea, and the 3rd Fleet was gaining ships and strength constantly, and Halsey was sure the fleet could interdict any Japanese troop landings.

Three marine divisions were in the South Pacific by this time, but only the 3rd Marine Division was available for the Bougainville operation. The 1st Marine Division was scheduled for the Cape Gloucester operation under General MacArthur, and the 2nd Marine Division had been moved to the Central Pacific area for the assault on the Gilbert Islands. But the 1st Marine Raider Regiment was available, and it would be used at Bougainville, along with the Army 25th Division. Particularly to be involved was the 2nd Marine Raider Battalion.

The marines were still not quite sure what they ought to do with the Raiders. Colonel Liversedge's 1st Marine Raider Regiment came out of the New Georgia campaign slated for some rest and rebuilding, since the battalions had suffered so many casualties and so much tropical sickness.

On September 12 a new 2nd Raider Regiment was established under the command of Lieutenant Colonel Alan Shapley, who had replaced Evans Carlson in command of the 2nd Raider Battalion.

The South Pacific was still "a poor relative" in the Allied military scheme. The Guadalcanal venture had been termed "Operation Shoestring" by Admiral Halsey, and now Bougainville was called "Operation Shoestring Number Two." Halsey was short of landing craft, of transports, of destroyer transports, particularly because the Gilberts invasion in the north, which was also scheduled for this November, would take a large number of ships.

At Bougainville the Allies would land, the marines first of all, establish a beachhead, and expand it, and then the army would take over. Airfield construction would start as soon as the landing was secure, for the purpose of this operation was to create airfields from which Rabaul could be attacked. The landings would be made on twelve beaches, by 13,900 men, and they would be unloaded along with their supplies and equipment in six hours. After that, for five days, LSTs would bring in supplies and troops at the rate of three thousand troops per day. The troops would build at least three bomber fields and two fighter fields, two of them to be established in a hurry.

So the 3rd Marine Division, which had been training in jungle warfare in Samoa and at Guadalcanal, was prepared for the landings. And attached to the division were the 2nd Raider Battalion and the 3rd Raider Battalion along with the 3rd Marine Defense Battalion. The 2nd Raider Battalion was attached to Task Unit A-1, which would land on six beaches near Cape Torokina. The 3rd Marine Raider Battalion was assigned to Task Unit A-2, which included the 9th Marine Regiment. The Raider Battalion would land on Puruata Island, which lies off Cape Torokina. It was to be a very frugal landing: so short of shipping was the command that it was ordained that the marines would land only with haversacks and fighting gear. Knapsacks and blanket rolls were to come ashore later; seabags, cots, and mattresses were not to come at all.

On October 30 the forces were assembled, the ships were loaded, and they began steaming toward a rendezvous point off Guadalcanal for the voyage up to Bougainville.

They called the force the Northern Landing Force. It arrived at Empress Augusta Bay shortly after dawn on November 1, after eight air alerts called this last night, during which night fighter planes chased away Japanese reconnaissance aircraft. General Quarters was sounded at five A.M., and as the sun came up the sharp peaks of Bougainville could be seen ahead. A thin mist hung over the island, and there were no Japanese aircraft to be seen, which meant that surprise had been achieved.

At 5:45 that morning the destroyer *Wadsworth* opened fire on the beaches north of Cape Torokina, and mine sweepers went to work. The *Wadsworth* moved inshore, within two miles of the beach, to fire on Japanese installations. When the sweepers reported no mines, the assault transports moved into the bay and shelled Puruata Island. At 6:45 the eight troop transports were inside, less than two miles from the shore, standing parallel to the shoreline. The destroyers *Anthony, Sigourney,* and *Wadsworth* fired five-inch shells into Puruata Island and the north beaches. The destroyer *Terry* fired on other beaches. While they bombarded the shore, the troops got into the landing craft. At 6:45 came the order to land the landing force, and the marines got down into the boats. The landing craft cast off from the ships and began to circle, awaiting the formation of their units. About 7,500 marines were preparing to land.

At 7:10 the barrage was shifted to another area, and five minutes later the first boats headed in toward the shore. At 7:21 fighters and bombers from the Munda airfield began to streak over the transports, bombing and strafing the beach ahead of the boats. The air attack lasted five minutes, and then stopped because the troops were hitting the beach. The Raiders were attached to Colonel Edward A. Craig's 8th Marines, which was to land on beaches Red 3, Red 2, Yellow 4, Red 1, and Yellow 3. From the sea the landings looked easy—there was no sign of serious Japanese resistance. But the sea was very rough, and the surf was extremely high, so high that LCMs and LCVPs were caught, tossed by the surf; some sank, and some were smashed together.

Marines began jumping overboard into chest-deep water, making their way to the narrow beach and the twelve-foot bank above it. But in spite of the troubles the troops made the landings, and by 7:50 parachute flares announced the fact to the ships offshore. The marines assembled and created a perimeter around their five beaches. They started to patrol, and set up an outpost on the west bank of the Laruma River. Other marines stayed on the beach to unload supplies. The landings continued to be rough. By mid-morning the battered remains of sixty-four LCVPs and twenty-two LCMs were scattered along the beaches.

That was the easy side. The hard side was shown on the six southern beaches—Yellow 2, Blue 2, Blue 3, Green 2, Yellow 1, Blue 1—and Green 1, the beach on Puruata Island, where the 2nd Marine Raider Battalion put foot down. Enemy resistance here began before the boats hit the beach. The 2nd and 3rd Battalions of the 3rd Marines landed south of the Koromokina River, under small-arms fire. The marines jumped out and sprinted for the jungle. They organized and began clearing the Japanese away. They wanted to make contact with the 2nd Raider Battalion on the right, but were prevented by a wide swamp.

The Raiders, under Major Richard T. Washburn, came under very heavy fire as they landed on Green Beach 2 to the right of Puruata. Two enemy bunkers were directly ahead of them, and thirty yards inland was a supporting trench line. Perhaps 125 Japanese defended this area. The Raiders organized quickly and set about blasting open the bunkers. As the explosives came in, the Japanese came out, and headed for the jungle. More raider boats came up, including that of Lieutenant Colonel Joseph W. McCaffery. They got ashore, but Colonel McCaffery was hit by Japanese fire and mortally wounded.

The Raiders and the 3rd Marines soon bogged down on the edge of the jungle. There were too many lagoons and too much swamp in back of that beach to let them do much reconnaissance. And the sniper fire was intense and deadly. But the Raiders began hunting those snipers and shooting them out of their trees. By eleven A.M. they had wiped out all organized enemy resistance from the bunker leftovers. The men of Raider Company M were assigned to set up a trail block on the old Mission Trail that led inland, and they moved out, passing the perimeter.

The hottest point in these landings was on the western side of Puruata Island. The 1st Battalion of the 3rd Marines was hit by crossfire as the boats rounded the western tip of the island. The fire came from Cape Torokina and from Puruata and Torokina islands. The boats moved into the extreme right side of the landing area, and the marines plunged to shore into the crossfire. Once the assault boats had come up to within five hundred yards of the shore, they were fired on by a concealed 75mm field gun. A shell hit the command boat and split it apart. The boat sank, and the boat group was thrown into the water. All coordination of the attack was then lost. The assault waves became confused; six boats were hit by this gun within a few minutes and only four of them made the beach. Then they faced Japanese mortar and machine-gun fire and rifle fire. On the beach were a number of concealed bunkers made of palm logs and sand, and these were connected by trenches. Once again the Japanese defenders had planned their bunkers well. They had interlocking fields of fire. The bunkers scarcely stood above the ground level, and they had completely withstood the bombardment by the destroyers and the air attacks by the bombers and fighters.

Against this fire there was nothing for the marines to do but run the gauntlet, get into the jungle, and then have time to reorganize. But there they came under mortar fire and the fire of the fifty-millimeter rifle grenade launchers, in whose use the Japanese infantrymen were very adept. On the island the marines were all mixed up; only Company B of the 1st Battalion of the 3rd Marines landed on the beach where it was supposed to go.

One of the problems was caused by a shrewd assessment by the Japanese defenders. They saw the LCI landing craft, larger than the others, and surmised that the American commanders would be aboard these craft, so they concentrated their fire on them. They were right, and they knocked out all semblance of unity by breaking up the command boats. Fourteen men were lost in sunken landing craft, and a dozen were killed on the beach in those first few minutes.

But in the protection of the bush the marines began to sort themselves out. Rifle groups were formed up along the shoreline, too, as the marines fought their way to widen the beachhead.

Fortunately the planning had been good on the squad levels. All units had been briefed on their missions, and each squad knew the missions of the other squads. Each marine had a sketched map of the Cape Torokina area and shoreline. So the marines pulled themselves together and began to attack the bunkers.

And as the Japanese had correctly assessed the marines' landing techniques, the marines had correctly assessed the Japanese defense tactics. They had studied the mutually protecting Japanese bunkers on New Georgia and decided that if they could crack one bunker, they could crack all the rest from that vantage point, moving from one to the next through the Japanese trenches. So they began: Browning automatic riflemen opened fire on the embrasures of a bunker. That kept the heads of the Japanese defenders down. Other marines then raced around to the blind side of the bunker and dropped grenades down the ventilators. Another marine covered the rear entrance, pouring fire into it if it opened.

Cape Torokina fell by mid-morning. That deadly 75mm gun was knocked out by a single marine, who crept up to the bunker where it was located, covered by the fire of his buddies, and sprayed the gun and gun crew with automatic fire. He fell dead from his wounds, but the gun crew was also dead.

The same was true of the other Torokina bunkers. After the fight was over, the marines counted 153 dead Japanese here. "Old Glory flies on Torokina Cape" was the message transmitted to the ships. "Situation well in hand."

On Puruata Island, Lieutenant Colonel Fred D. Beans's 3rd Raider Battalion seemed to have an easy landing. One reinforced company made the initial assault, with the rest of the battalion in reserve. As the boats came in to the island, they drew sporadic gunfire. But they landed, and by 9:30 they had established a perimeter about 125 yards inland. The trouble again was snipers and well-directed fire from hidden machine guns and mortars. The going was very rough. At

1:30 Colonel Beans committed his reserves to the attack. They got several self-propelled 75mm guns from the 9th Marines, and began to move. Soon they were about halfway across the island. But the sniper fire continued and the Japanese retreated reluctantly, so the fighting continued. As night fell, the marines formed a perimeter and dug in.

Next morning just after dawn, the marines launched a two-pronged attack. The Japanese seemed to be running low on ammunition because the firing slowed down and finally was reduced to sporadic rifle fire. By 3:30 in the afternoon of the second day the Japanese had been eliminated from the island. Twenty-nine bodies were found; the remainder of the estimated hundred defenders had escaped to the main island of Bougainville. The 3rd Raiders had lost five men killed and thirty-two wounded. But they were ashore, the beachhead was secured, and the Japanese had not launched any effective counterattack on that second day. The battle for Bougainville had begun.

—20—

The Beachhead

When the fighting was at its height, the Japanese reacted sharply. Two hours after the transports and cargo ships appeared off Cape Torokina, a large flight of Japanese planes was seen coming in toward the invasion fleet. The transports pulled away from the beaches to get to sea and take evasive action. The first planes to come in consisted of about thirty fighters from Rabaul. They were intercepted by a New Zealand fighter squadron that was flying cover for the invasion fleet, but the fighters stuck to their mission and came in strafing the beaches and the transports. The New Zealanders went after the Zeros, and knocked down seven of them. Ten minutes later came another Japanese air attack, this time bombers escorted by fighters. They bombed the transports and the beaches, but the ships outmaneuvered the bombs. The destroyer *Wadsworth* was very nearly hit, and the shrapnel from a bomb caused several casualties. The enemy air attackers were hard hit, this time by American marine fighter planes, and eight Japanese planes were shot down. The air attacks then stopped for a time. The transports came back to the beaches and unloaded more supplies. But later in the day a formation of about seventy Japanese planes came in to attack, and the transports again stood out to sea. One transport, the *American Legion*, grounded on a reef and remained there but was finally pulled off by two tugs.

On the beaches in mid-afternoon the marines had a chance to look over the Japanese defenses they had conquered. They found them very strong, much stronger than they had appeared on the aerial photographs taken before the invasion. So little had been known because the Japanese were masterful at the arts of camouflage. Cape Torokina, for example, had been ringed by fifteen bunkers, nine of them facing west and six facing east. Inside this protective line was another ring of eight bunkers, whose fields of fire covered the fifteen bunkers, and inside this second ring were two more bunkers, which covered the others.

The bunkers were built of ironwood, and coconut logs two feet thick. The logs were buttressed by sandbags, and they were built so low above the ground that they were barely visible. They were also covered with sand and brush. In the day's fighting, twenty of the bunkers had been broken down by marines hurling grenades and satchel charges inside. The other five had been destroyed much more simply by the 75mm self-propelled guns that had been brought in.

By late afternoon of this first day at Bougainville the marine defense perimeter stretched in a semi-circle from the Laruma River, about four miles, to the other side of Cape Torokina. Japanese snipers were still shooting around the cape, but the work had to go on nonetheless.

The immediate problem was not the snipers or the small groups of Japanese in the jungles outside the marine perimeter but the conditions within the perimeter itself. The northern beaches were full of the wreckage of landing craft, and were unusable, so they were abandoned, and all cargo for the 9th Marines was delivered to the beaches south of the Koromokina River. This meant that the Raiders' beaches were extremely crowded. And when the marines tried to extend the perimeter inland so they could establish supply dumps, they found the ground too marshy to handle vehicles. So the supplies had to be stored just off the beaches, above the high-water mark. The 3rd Raider Battalion's beach on Puruata Island was stacked as more landing craft were diverted there, and the supplies kept coming in even when the fighting on the island was at its height.

By the end of D-Day most of the supplies were unloaded. Four transports still had supplies aboard, but they were sent to sea and then brought back so they would arrive at Empress Augusta Bay early in the morning. The perimeter of the marines extended into the jungle six hundred yards near the Laruma River, and one thousand yards near Cape Torokina. The sounds of rifle fire could still be heard on Puruata Island, where the 3rd Raider Battalion were still chasing down snipers. But slowly some order was beginning to appear.

The 12th Marines—the artillery—were moving into position to support various elements of the perimeter.

The battery that supported the 2nd Raider Battalion was having some troubles; it had to move inland a hundred yards, through a lagoon, to find a position for the guns. Two amphibious tractors carried the guns and ammunition across the lagoon. The artillerymen brought more ammunition and food across in rubber boats. The battery then registered in on Piva Village, guided by air spotters. This village was a Japanese stronghold, from which counterattacks could be expected.

As night fell, the Raiders manned their foxholes along the perimeter, three men to a foxhole, one man to be on watch at all times. The orders were that there was to be no unnecessary firing of weapons during the night. They were to rely on bayonets and trench knives if the enemy attacked, and any infiltrators were to be ignored. If they managed to get inside the perimeter, they would be dealt with at dawn. The night passed as the Raiders expected, with infiltrators trying to come through the perimeter. It began to rain, and the drizzle continued all night long. The Japanese came, but not in a banzai attack. Some marines remained untroubled, but others found themselves fighting with trench knives to keep the Japanese out of their foxholes.

That night a Japanese task force of four cruisers and six destroyers was reported coming down from Truk toward Rabaul. Admiral Koga, the successor to Admiral Yamamoto, was sending elements of the Combined Fleet down to make an attack on Bougainville. It could be expected to arrive the next day. Rear Admiral Aaron S. Merrill was bringing Task Force 39, the American cruiser and destroyer force, up to Bougainville to engage the enemy when the time came.

It came after midnight. Task Force 39 engaged the

enemy. The battle was strung out and confused, but at the end the Americans had one destroyer disabled by a torpedo and several other ships hit by shells, including the cruiser *Denver*. The Japanese lost a light cruiser and a destroyer, and several other ships were damaged. The victory was American, because the Japanese ships withdrew without shelling the beach-head.

At daybreak on D + 1 the marines began to expand the perimeter. The Raiders sent out patrols to deal with the snipers on Puruata Island. They found that the terrain was more trouble than the Japanese, a maze of swamps, whose bottoms were volcanic ash that behaved like quicksand.

There were two trails through the area; one was the Mission trail, which led to the Piva River and Piva Village, and this was blocked by Company M of the Raiders. The 2nd Raider Battalion stood fast. On the third day the marines were still receiving fire from Torokina Island, so the artillery worked that area over, and then the 3rd Raiders sent a detachment to check up. The Raiders found no live Japanese, but ten graves. The artillery fire had forced the Japanese to abandon Torokina Island, obviously.

The 2nd Raiders moved out along the Mission trail and extended the beachhead about 1,500 yards. Something new was added, a war-dog platoon of marines with Doberman pinscher and German shepherd dogs that had been trained to smell out the enemy. When the Raiders discovered that the system really worked, it was a great boon to morale.

On November 5, the 2nd and 3rd Raider Battalions, except for Company M, which was blocking the Mission trail, began to assemble on Puruata Island and

Cape Torokina, in reserve. Lieutenant Colonel Alan Shapley was in command. Soon the 2nd Raider Battalion moved up the trail from the Buretoni Mission toward the Piva River. This was the main link between the Torokina area and the Numa Numa trail, which led south to the area of strength of the Japanese army. On the night of November 5, the men of Company E of the Raiders were manning the trail block, when the Japanese mounted an attack. The Raiders drove off two attacks that night, but a certain number of Japanese got through and headed toward the marine perimeter. The next day Lieutenant Colonel Shapley moved the 2nd and 3rd Raider Battalions up to the block in anticipation of a strong Japanese attack that night.

Nothing happened overnight, but the Japanese in the south were obviously in contact with Rabaul, and knew that something was about to happen. The something was a counterlanding by Japanese troops from Rabaul. But once again General Imamura at Rabaul underestimated the American strength as he had at Guadalcanal. He thought there were only about five thousand marines ashore on Bougainville, so he sent a landing force of less than a thousand men to wipe them out. They were to attack from the sea, while troops from the south were to break through along the Piva trail, to join them and create a pincer that would squeeze the marines.

On the beach, the 3rd Marines and the 9th Marines were facing that Japanese counterlanding in the Laruma River area on November 7. About eight hundred troops from Rabaul made the landing. They got ashore near the Laruma River just outside the marine perimeter.

That afternoon the Japanese from the south came

up to attack the Raider roadblock. Company H had just moved into position, replacing Company F, which had manned the position the night before. About two hundred Japanese made the charge. The Raiders of Company H opened fire with machine guns, automatic rifles, and rifles. Shapley rushed up a platoon from Company E and all of Company G. They were supported by 81mm mortars in the rear. The mortars did the trick, and the Japanese attack slowed and finally fizzled out. The Japanese withdrew and dug in at Piva village, a half mile away.

As the afternoon wore on, several small units of Japanese tried to infiltrate through the roadblock, but in each case they were beaten back, and no Japanese got through. That night the Japanese made a major attempt to force their way. It was preceded by heavy 90mm mortar fire on Company G of the Raiders, which was manning the roadblock. Then the Japanese infantry began moving up. The Raiders stayed in their foxholes, as ordered, and did not fire until the Japanese were in point-blank range. Then they let loose a withering fire that forced the Japanese to withdraw. One marine was killed. The Japanese took away their own dead, so the marines did not know how many had fallen. Down on the beach, the 9th Marines were fighting the Japanese counterlanding troops. The 3rd Battalion of the 9th Marines attacked the Japanese that morning of November 7. The fighting was brisk, but the Japanese did not get through to Piva as they had hoped. However, several marine units were cut off by the enemy and had to fight their way back to the lines.

On the morning of November 8 the 1st Battalion of the 21st Marines attacked on the beach area after an artillery barrage. The attack was led by light tanks. It overwhelmed the Japanese, and the marines killed about 250 of them.

On the trail that morning, Company M of the 3rd Raiders hurried up to relieve Company H, which had done the bulk of the fighting the night before. Company G took over the trail block. Company M went into position behind the trailblockers with two platoons on the left and one platoon on the right side of the trail. They waited for the attack they knew was coming.

Two Japanese battalions attacked this time after a heavy mortar barrage. By eleven A.M. the marines were fighting all along this line. Company G, which was astride trail, took the point of the attack. Actually there was no real need to worry about being outflanked. The ground on both sides of the trail, after a few yards, petered out into marshland. The Japanese did try two times, but each time they bogged down in the swamp and were picked off by the marine riflemen.

At one P.M. the Japanese attack was stalled and the 2nd Raider Battalion tried a counterattack. Company F and Company E began a flanking movement from the right side of the line. They struggled through the swamp. But they had not gone fifty yards when they ran into a large force of Japanese, and the fight for possession of the trail began again.

The Japanese tried to break through in a frontal attack on Company G at the trail block. The American machine guns mowed them down. The Americans brought up half tracks and two tanks, but they proved to be almost useless in the swampy ground. Their major use was to evacuate the wounded.

By four o'clock that afternoon the struggle had

become stalemated. The marines could not move forward, and the Japanese could not pass the roadblock. Another Japanese banzai charge was turned back, but it was noticed that this one had a lot less fervor than the earlier ones.

With darkness coming, the Raiders were ordered back to their previous positions and they began to move out. Company F covered the disengagement. The Raiders counted casualties: eight men killed and twenty-seven wounded. They estimated that 125 Japanese had been killed that day on the trail.

That night Major General Allen H. Turnage decided that the marines had to clear the enemy away from the trail block and ordered an attack. It would be made by the 2nd Raider Battalion with the support of tanks and half tracks.

At 7:30 on the morning of November 9 the artillery began bombarding the Japanese positions on the trail on the other side of the marine trail block. Some eight hundred rounds were fired, some of them within 250 yards of the Raiders' positions. But at the same time the Japanese had moved forward to establish their own position on the trail about one hundred yards from the Raider position, with both flanks protected by impassable swamp. The Japanese began firing machine guns and rifles at the marines.

The Raider attack began at eight A.M. Company L was supposed to move up the left side of the trail; Company F would move up the right side. But when the command came to get moving, only half of Company F started, although Company L was attacking as ordered. The two companies lost touch and did not regain it. The Japanese fired "knee mortars," those very effective rifle grenade launchers, and machine guns. The American tanks and half tracks could not come up along the narrow corridor, and they could not come up through the swamps on the flanks. The entire American attack was straight frontal assault. But by 9:30 the superior firepower of the larger American rifles and Browning automatic rifles and .50-caliber machine guns began to tell. The Raiders began to gain ground. The Japanese tried to counterattack up the center, between companies L and F, but Colonel Craig, who was directing the attack himself, brought up Company K of the Raiders and the Weapons Company of the 9th Marines. By 12:30 the Japanese saw that they could not break through the American line, and suddenly the major elements withdrew back up the Piva trail. The Raiders found the going easy, they were facing only stragglers and snipers. They developed a new technique of dealing with snipers—the use of the machine gun to spray the foliage of the trees, knocking down snipers they had never seen up there. It became standard practice in dealing with snipers. The Raiders did not find any Japanese on either trail. They did find a large bivouac area on the Numa Numa trail, but it was abandoned. The Japanese had retreated to the south. The battle was over, won by the marines. They counted a hundred Japanese dead. They had lost twelve men killed and thirty wounded.

—21—

The Battle of Piva Forks

On November 10, 1943, the marines had planned an
air strike against the Japanese who might be lurking
along the Piva trail. But the strike had to be delayed
when it was discovered that a patrol from Company K
of the 3rd Raider Battalion had not come back from a
mission into Piva village. Finally in broad daylight the
patrol showed up to report that it had not made any
contacts with the enemy. The air strike was delivered
just before ten A.M., and then the marines began
moving up on Piva village.

The 9th Marines led the way, the Raiders having
been moved into reserve following their heavy fighting
of the past few days. They bivouacked within the
perimeter and rested. They had played a major role in
the defeat of the Japanese counterlanding attempt and
the further efforts of the Japanese to link up from the
south with that Rabaul group. About a thousand Japa-

nese had been killed in that attempted mousetrap play by General Imamura.

Two days after the successful battle of the road-block, the marines moved to begin building the first airfield, which was the purpose of the whole Bougainville operation. A site was selected midway between the Koromokina and Piva rivers. The problem was that this site was a mile out in front of the 3rd Marine Division's perimeter. Therefore General Turnage decided that another attack must be made to extend the area of control and establish a combat outpost that could sustain itself. So on November 12 the 21st Marines were ordered into the line. They were fresh from Guadalcanal.

At 6:30 on the morning of November 13 the 21st Marines moved up to try to capture the junction of the Numa Numa trail and the East-West trail. But the 2nd Battalion of the 21st Marines was inexperienced, and the Japanese beat them to the trail junction located in a coconut grove. The marines began to take heavy casualties, and made no progress in their attack. Company E and Company F, in the front of the line, suddenly found themselves in a critical position with the Japanese threatening to break through. Communications failed and the marines withdrew from the coconut grove. Company F had gotten itself behind the Japanese lines and was in danger of being wiped out. At 6:30 that night the 2nd Raider Battalion was rudely yanked out of bivouac and sent forward to save the day. The Raiders got into position along the trail and protected the lines of communication that night. The next morning, after an air strike and some fumbling on the ground, the 21st Marines began to organize, buttressed by the Raiders. The marines moved forward, first haltingly, and then with more confidence. The Japanese positions in the coconut grove were overrun. Mop-up operations continued until 3:30 that afternoon. When the marines counted, they found forty Japanese dead. But this time the casualty rate was higher for the Americans: twenty men had been killed, including five officers, and thirty-nine marines had been wounded. The 2nd Battalion of the 21st Marines had learned much in those two days of fighting, and they had been saved from disaster by the 2nd Raider Battalion.

Soon the first troops of the army's 37th Division began coming ashore. They were supposed to take over the garrison duties on Bougainville, but it was apparent that more than garrison activity was still going to be needed. The Japanese were far from finished, and their force in the south, the troops of the 6th Division, might have made a major attack at any time. So although the Raiders had done their job, and expected to be pulled out of the Empress Augusta Bay area, it was not to be just yet. Lieutenant Colonel Shapley's 2nd Marine Raider Regiment was drawn out of the line and put in reserve for a little rest. But even as the Raiders came out they knew they would be back in again. They were the ready reserve, to be used to plug up any holes in the perimeter or for quick reinforcement of an attack or front line defense.

The building of roads and bridges, and the construction of two airfields, began, the way led by the 3rd Amphibian Tractor Battalion with its amtracs, which could negotiate the endless mud and swamp.

The next few days were spent in reorganizing the perimeter to accommodate the incoming army troops.

Then on November 17 the enemy reappeared along the Numa Numa trail and the fighting began once again. The 3rd Marines, who had been moved up to replace the Raiders, were tired, and so the 3rd Raider Battalion was brought up to replace the 3rd Battalion of the 3rd Marines. The objective was to be the new Japanese position on the Numa Numa trail. The 3rd Battalion of the 3rd Marines was then assigned to take that position. There would be no rest just now for them either. They moved up and the Raiders came up to support them. The 3rd Battalion of the 3rd Marines and the army's 129th Infantry were carrying the attack, but they were getting into trouble—a gap had appeared between the army and marine troops, and the 3rd Raider Battalion was rushed to the gap. They crossed the Piva River and moved to a hill known as Cibik's Hill, after the major who had taken it during a patrol. The Raiders relieved the 3rd Battalion of the 3rd Marines there. On November 23 the marines were in position to attack the next day along the East-West trail, about eight hundred yards beyond the east fork of the Piva River.

The battle now changed on both sides. For the first time the Japanese brought up artillery to shell the American positions. They also shelled Torokina and the beaches where some LSTs were unloading. Scouts had estimated that the enemy force was located around the village of Kogubikopai-ai, and that the Japanese numbered about 1,500.

The Americans brought up seven battalions of artillery and all sort of machine guns, including captured Japanese machine guns, into the line on Cibik's ridge, in preparation for the coming battle. By nightfall of the twenty-third, the marines had forty-four machine guns in place and dozens of 81mm and 60mm mortars.

Then came November 24. It was Thanksgiving Day, but there was no celebration on Bougainville. The marines were eating K rations, not turkey, and throwing away the hardtack that came with it, drinking water laced with chlorine tablets, to take down their bitter Atabrine pills, and getting ready for the new fight.

At 8:30 in the morning the seven battalions of artillery opened fire on the Japanese positions in front of the 32nd Marines. The barrage lasted for twenty minutes, and sixty tons of 75mm and 105mm and mortar shells were shot at the enemy. Then, just before the marines were to move, the Japanese began shelling with such accuracy that there was some talk about calling off the attack. But the observers on Cibik's ridge spotted a forward Japanese battery on the slope of a small coconut grove not far from the Piva River. The enemy battery was quickly destroyed, and the marines began to move. They eased through a forest that was as still as death, for death was all around them. The forward Japanese positions had been blasted to pieces. The gray-green–clad bodies of Japanese snipers hung awkwardly from the trees where they had been roped in, and on the ground the bodies were thick around the wreckage of the positions. But after a few hundred yards the Japanese in the rear areas began to recover and to fight back. Enemy artillery fell among the marines, and enemy mortars blasted their line of advance. The fighting was heavy on the right of the East-West trail and one battalion reported seventy casualties in a move of 250 yards. The marines had to cross a small stream eight times, and they found at least three Japanese pillboxes at each bend in the stream. Fortunately for them their new equipment for attack included flamethrowers wielded by engineers. The Japanese soon got the message, and concentrated their fire on the flamethrowers, trying to kill the engineers before they could get close to the bunkers.

The marines reached their first objectives at about noon. They rested and started forward again. The artillery made all the difference; the marines just kept going despite heavy resistance. When the advance ended that day the marines counted more than one thousand dead Japanese. The marines had 115 dead and wounded.

And that night there was a Thanksgiving dinner. A large shipment of turkeys reached the beachhead. The division cooks scrubbed out fifty-gallon oil drums, boiled all the turkeys, and sent them up front. Almost all the marines of the front line ate their turkey dinner that night. It was just like home, if you lived in a foxhole, with people shooting at you all night long.

On November 25 the tired 3rd Marines were taken out of the line. They were replaced by the 1st Battalion of the 9th Marines, with the 2nd Battalion of the Raider regiment and two companies of the 3rd Raiders. That day they took over the front line once again. They moved out along the East-West trail with the 9th Marines to start the attack of the day. The 2nd Raiders were on the left flank on a front of eight hundred yards. At ten A.M., after another artillery barrage, the attack was started down Cibik's ridge. The 2nd Raiders were held up several times by machine-gun emplacements, but the Japanese gave ground slowly. That night the 2nd Raiders obtained their objective, and so did the 9th Marines, except for one hill called Grenade Hill, which held out all day. But the next morning the marines discovered that the Japanese had withdrawn from Grenade Hill during the night. That day, November 26, the marines moved forward and controlled the ridge line which had blocked the East-West trail.

After the fighting of November 26, the exhausted 3rd Marines were moved from the front line into reserve. They were back near Cape Torokina, with twenty-seven days of jungle fighting behind them. But the Raiders stayed on. On November 29, Raiders of Company M of the 3rd Raider Battalion joined Major Richard Fagan's 1st Parachute Battalion in a raid on the Japanese lines in the southern part of Empress Augusta Bay to prevent an enemy counterattack from that area. Early on the morning of the twenty-ninth the Raiders and the paratroops embarked on LCMs and LCVPs at Cape Torokina, and at four A.M. the craft moved toward Koiari Beach. The marines landed in what turned out to be the middle of a Japanese supply dump. They were greeted by a Japanese officer wearing a sword, who thought they were reinforcements. The surprise was mutual and the marines jumped ashore and began digging in. Before the Japanese recovered, the parachute troops and Raiders had pushed out a perimeter that extended 350 yards along the beach and 180 yards inland. But the force was split and most of the Raiders were outside the dump area. The Japanese began shelling with 90mm mortars. Periodically they staged a banzai charge. Life was getting rough. Major Fagan radioed back to the headquarters of the amphibious command, now under Major General Geiger, and suggested that the marines be withdrawn. Geiger was willing, but when he planned a rescue attempt the radios of Fagan's men failed and they did not get the message. But by this time, 9:30 in the morning, at least the marines consolidated their position when the Raiders fought their way up to join the main body.

The Japanese force numbered about 1,200 men and their positions for fighting were much better than those of the marines. The marines from Torokina tried to rescue the Raiders and parachute troops with landing craft, but the attempt was beaten off by Japanese artillery fire. So was a second attempt. Late in the afternoon the marines heard Japanese trucks coming up from the south and guessed that they would receive a very powerful attack that night. The Raiders and the parachutists were in bad shape; they had their backs to the sea, and they were low on ammunition. Their chances of survival did not seem good.

But at Cape Torokina, the marine artillery of the 3rd Defense Battalion registered along the northern perimeter of the marine raiding unit, and that protected them from attack from that direction. General Geiger sent a message to the navy, which was escorting some ships back to Guadalcanal, and three destroyers were detached and sent with an LCI gunboat. They were the *Fullam, Lansdowne,* and *Lardner*. They arrived just before dusk and opened fire on the Japanese. The destroyers fired on the flanks of the marines, while the 155mm guns on Torokina fired parallel to the beach. The effect was to create a box, with the sea at the back of the marines, and protect them from attack by the Japanese. Now the landing craft made a dash for the beach. They came just in time. The marines were almost entirely out of ammunition, and protected from a banzai charge only by the destroyers and the guns of the 3rd Marine Defense Battalion.

Here is the report in the official history of the marines:

As the rescue boats beached, the marines slowly retired toward the shore. There was no stampede, no panic. The withdrawal was orderly and deliberate. After waiting to insure that all marines were off the perimeter, the battalion commander gave the signal to clear the beach, and at 2040 (8:40 P.M.) the last boat pulled away without drawing a single enemy shot. The artillery battery and the gunfire support ships then worked over the entire beach, hoping to destroy the Japanese force by random fires.

The attempt to raid the Japanese system of communications and supply along the Bougainville coast ended in a dismal failure. Although the marines had landed in an area where great destruction could have been accomplished, they were never able to do more than hug the shoreline and attempt to defend their meagre toehold with dwindling ammunition until rescued. In the pitch darkness at the time of evacuation much of the marine equipment was lost. Although the withdrawal was orderly, some of the weapons, rifles, and packs were left behind. Enemy supplies destroyed would have to be credited to the bombardment by Allied artillery and destroyers after the evacuation. The marines estimated that the Japanese had lost about 291 men, about half of whom were probably killed and the others wounded. The marine parachute battalion, which landed with a total of 24 officers and 505 enlisted men, plus four officers and 80 enlisted men from the 3rd Raiders, listed casualties of 15 killed or died of wounds, 99 wounded, and seven missing.

So that aspect of the battle for Bougainville ended, and the Japanese were still well in control of the island, save for the enclave around Empress Augusta Bay, where the Americans were building air strips to be used in the attack on Rabaul.

At the end of November one major problem remained: a hill mass a little over a mile from the lines which dominated the area between the Piva and Torokina rivers. This hill could give the Japanese an observation point from which to watch all of Cape Torokina and a position from which to launch an attack against the beachhead. General Geiger thought the whole ridge line ought to be occupied, so the parachutists and the Raiders were moved toward these hills. By the end of December 5 the parachute regiment, the Raiders, and the men of the 3rd, 9th, and 21st Marines, had established an outpost line from Hill 1000 in this mass to the junction of the East-West trail at the Torokina River. At just about this time the Japanese suddenly discovered that they wanted these positions, and they began to move. On December 5 the Japanese ambushed an American patrol of the 9th Marines. From that point on the fighting continued almost constantly, fighting for these hills. They fought on December 8. They fought on December 9. The Japanese seemed to be growing in strength, which indicated something to the marines. On the night of December 9 several marine patrols were ambushed around Hill 1000. The next day the parachute regiment was hit by a very strong Japanese counterattack aimed at the center of the positions on Hill 1000. The marine artillery saved the day, throwing in 75mm and 105mm howitzer shells until the Japanese attack was scattered. But the parachutists had been hard hit: they lost twelve men killed and twenty-six wounded in this very short fight. The big problem that day was getting the wounded down the hill. The rain had been coming down in torrents, so the two trails were impassable. It took twelve men to handle each stretcher case and get the wounded man down the hill to the aid station on the rear slope.

The next day the whole area was reinforced by the 21st Marines. The parachute troops and Raiders moved out into reserve. But the fighting continued and the area got a new name, Hellzapoppin Ridge, because of the almost constant activity against the Japanese for the next week. On December 13, when artillery and all else had failed to dislodge the Japanese from their side of the ridge, General Geiger called for air support. Six planes were flown to the Torokina air strip for operations. They bombed the area. Actually four of them bombed the Japanese with 100-pound fragmentation bombs and the other plane bombed the marines, killing two men and wounding five. In spite of this error, the marines requested another strike for the next day. That next day seventeen planes struck, and they hit the Japanese. And the following day, December 15, they did the same. There were more air strikes on December 18, and the marines made an assault on Hellzapoppin Ridge just afterward. They captured the ridge after some fierce fighting. But the Japanese had simply moved back to Hill 600 and once again the marines faced the same problem. For several days they fought for Hill 600. Then, one night, in that inexplicable (to the marines) fashion of the Japanese, they suddenly moved out, and left the area to the Americans. The reason was simple enough: they were short of ammunition and food, and their commanders saw that they would not conquer. The Japanese moved across the Torokina River and south.

So the perimeter was under control and the airfield construction could continue apace. It seemed likely that the army occupation troops could now take over from the marines, and on the 27th of December Major General John R. Hodge brought the Americal Division in to become the garrison. The whole 3rd Marine Division was returned to Guadalcanal—except the Raiders and the parachute battalion. For insurance against a surprise Japanese attack they were kept on the island of Bougainville for two more weeks. They manned the right flank of the area, along the Torokina River, for it was from here that a Japanese attack would have to come, since the enemy were in the south. They shipped out after two more weeks, and then the only marines left were the men of the 3rd Defense Battalion and they stayed on until June. The Raiders went back to Guadalcanal. They counted noses again. The 2nd Marine Raider Regiment had lost 64 men killed and 204 men wounded in the Bougainville campaign, or about fourteen percent of the total 1,841 casualties. Considering the fact that the Raiders had participated in virtually all the important actions, their casualty rate was low, and gave an indication of the value of the training they had received.

—22—

To the Fourth Marines

The 2nd Raider Regiment returned to Guadalcanal
after the job had been done and the airstrips had been
established on Bougainville at Empress Augusta Bay.
The Pacific command did not know quite what to do
with them after that. The fact is that by this time the
Raiders were the subject of controversy. The Marine
Corps resented Admiral Kelly Turner's attempt to
interfere and establish what seemed to others to be a
private army. Indeed, the 2nd Raider Battalion had
been called "Nimitz's Private Army" when it showed
up at Pearl Harbor in 1942. And in the autumn of 1943
there was another reason for controversy, which came
after the invasion of the Gilbert Islands, the first step
in the march across the Central Pacific toward Japan.

The Japanese had seized control of the Gilberts on
December 10, 1941, from Great Britain, but they did
nothing much with them. The Gilberts seemed to them

to be useful only as observation posts for the Pacific. Then, when in August 1942 Lieutenant Colonel Evans Carlson's 2nd Raider Battalion had made its raid on Makin, the Japanese began to reconsider. Imperial General Headquarters took the position that the Makin raid was an attempt to force the Japanese to reinforce the islands in order to draw troops away from the South Pacific. But Imperial General Headquarters also recognized the vulnerability of these islands to attack, and the possibility of the Americans launching an attack on them. So the decision was made in 1942 to build up the defenses of the Gilberts.

In May 1943 Japanese admirals conferred at Truk and adopted the Z Plan. Changes were needed in view of the loss of Guadalcanal, the struggle for New Guinea, and the attack that was beginning on New Georgia. This plan established an outer perimeter that ran from the Aleutian Islands through the Gilbert and Marshall islands, to the Bismarck Islands. If the Americans made any attempts along this line, the fleet would challenge them and the island garrisons would defend to the last. If, for example, the Americans attacked the Gilberts, Japanese bombers from the Bismarcks would attack the convoys, land at fields in the Gilberts and Marshalls, rearm and refuel, and attack again. At the same time, fighters and short-range bombers would attack from Truk and other bases.

This plan was reviewed in September 1943, and was modified somewhat. The Gilberts, which had not been fortified at all, would now be fortified heavily and the center of the defense would be the island of Betio, and there, under Admiral Keiji Shibasaki, pillboxes and blockhouses were built with interlocking fields of fire, and twenty coast defense guns, automatic weapons, and all sorts of obstacles to the landing forces. On the beach, concrete tetrahedrons forced the landing troops into patterns that would let the defenders sweep their boats with gunfire. Perhaps a hundred machine guns and smaller field pieces could sweep the beaches. The beaches themselves were protected by double apron strings of barbed wire. It was the Japanese hope that the invading troops would be stopped at the water's edge. But if they made it to the beach, then they faced a log fence, antitank ditches, and many other obstacles. And if the troops got farther ashore, then they faced the big bunkers and blockhouses made of reinforced concrete so strong that they could withstand direct hits by bombs or naval gunfire.

The invasion of the Gilberts came on November 19, 1943. How times had changed! Red Mike Edson was now a full colonel and chief of staff of the 2nd Marine Division. Lieutenant Colonel Carlson was now an observer, reporting to Colonel David M. Shoup of the 2nd Marines. At noon on D-Day at Betio, Lieutenant Colonel Carlson took a landing craft from the beach out to the battleship *Maryland* to report to Major General Julian Smith, the commander of the invasion troops, to tell him what was happening on the beachhead. What was happening was dreadful. The Japanese defenses were the toughest the marines had yet encountered. The difficulties were so great that Carlson even interrupted his mission. He saw a number of marines from the 3rd Battalion of the 8th Marines who were stranded on a pier, having been dumped out of their landing craft. He brought several loads of infantrymen from the pier to Betio, and brought wounded men out to boats at the reef line. He did not get to see General Smith until after six P.M.

The fighting was intense, the casualties were very high. On D+1 Lieutenant Colonel Carlson was still serving as Colonel Shoup's liaison officer. He had spent the night aboard the *Maryland*, but in the morning he went back to Betio to find Colonel Shoup in the shadow of an enemy bunker about thirty yards inland. Shoup informed him that the troops were short of water and ammunition, and Carlson offered to help organize the supply situation. And then he began planning. His first idea was to use the LVTs (amtracs) to bring supplies inland, and then to bring the wounded out to the ships. Then he had to find the LVTs. He went out to the minesweeper *Pursuit* and got eighteen LVTs assigned to the job. Then he went out to the *Maryland* again to confer with Red Mike Edson, the chief of staff of the division, about what was happening ashore.

On this second day, the 2nd Marine Division began to make progress. Red Mike said that at about 12:30 things broke rapidly, and the tide of battle shifted fast. Colonel Edson went ashore at 8:30 that night and took command of the troops. The next morning, November 22, the marines began to attack successfully, driving against the bunkers and routing the Japanese. And on the fourth day, November 23, Betio was secured by the marines. Of the estimated 4,300 Japanese troops and Korean laborers on the island, only 146 surrendered and only 17 of these were Japanese. The defenders died with their boots on.

When Major General Holland M. Smith contemplated the fighting in the Gilberts after it was all over, he was bitter about the raid made by Carlson's Raiders

on the Gilberts the year before. He said it was the
cause of the high casualty rate, because the raid had
tipped the Japanese off that the Americans were considering an attack on the Gilberts and they strengthened their defenses accordingly. General Smith could
see nothing of intelligence value in the Carlson raid
that would have justified the maneuver. The fact was
that the decision was not Carlson's or any other marine's but Admiral Nimitz's and his chief of staff. They
wanted to see how they might make use of this new
unit of shock troops; the raid was not strictly necessary at all, but was an experiment. The fact that it
turned out to be a disastrous one was not the fault of
the Raiders, but it left its mark nonetheless. For it
provided ammunition to those in the Marine Corps
who wanted to disband the Raider regiments and eliminate the whole concept. The idea was given further
credence when the China Lobby, representing Chiang
Kaishek's nationalist government in America, supported this view. The China Lobby was extremely
jealous of any good publicity given the Chinese communists, and Evans Carlson and the movie *Carlson's
Raiders* was an enormous publicity plus for the Chinese communists. In Congress and elsewhere the ru-
mor spread that somehow Carlson's Raiders and their
"gung-ho" concept were un-American. The marines
did not like that either. One result was the end of the
line for Evans Carlson's career. Red Mike Edson's
career was proceeding very well, and he had been
Carlson's equal in the command of the first two Raider
Battalions. But Carlson's career ended and he was
never promoted above the rank of Lieutenant Colonel
and he never had another command.

The second result of the bad publicity for the Marine

Corps was the definite decision to disband the Raider regiments, and take the four Raider battalions as the nucleus of a new marine regiment. Thus was created the new 4th Marines, under the command of Colonel Alan Shapley. It was apparent then that the 4th Marines would carry on the traditions of the Raiders. The 1st Raider Battalion became the 1st Battalion of the 4th Marines. The 3rd Raider Battalion became the 2nd Battalion. The 4th Raider Battalion became the 3rd Battalion of the 4th Marines, and the 2nd Raider Battalion became the Regimental Weapons Company. An artillery battalion was transferred from the 3rd Marines, and special troops were also attached. So the 4th Marines were set up to continue to fight the Pacific war. The first action of the new regiment was the capture of Emirau Island, a bit of coral four miles long and half a mile wide. It was important only because of its location, seventy-five miles from Kavieng, an important Japanese base, and the big Japanese naval base at Truk. With Emirau, and the bases at Bougainville captured with the help of the Raiders, the Allies would be able to squeeze Rabaul out of the war and let it wither on the vine.

The marines were looking for trouble when the mission was announced. The task force would be headed by Brigadier General A. H. Noble, and the 4th Marines were told about it only thirty-six hours before they were to take off. Colonel Shapley and his staff sweated out the period, poring over maps and getting all the information they could. But when the invasion came off, the 4th Marines were greeted by friendly natives, all of them Seventh Day Adventists. It happened on March 1, 1944, and because there was no fighting the capture was called "the jawbone campaign." One patrol of the 4th Marines went to St. Matthias Island, twelve miles northwest of Emirau, and captured that place just after the forty-six-man Japanese garrison left by dugout canoe. By the middle of March the whole operation was over, and the 4th Marines went back to the old Raider quarters on Guadalcanal to await a new assignment.

The new assignment was something else: the recapture of Guam. But first the 4th Marines and their Raider officers were made a part of the 1st Provisional Marine Brigade.

—23—
Guam

Many of the faces were the same, but the unit numbers were different. The leaders of the Marine Corps knew in choosing the Raiders to make up the 4th Marine Regiment that they were not going to miss; these men were apt successors to the heroes of the old 4th Marines, the "China Regiment" whose commander, Colonel Samuel L. Howard, had burned the colors on May 6, 1942, when the regiment had to surrender at Corregidor because President Roosevelt had opted against sending help to the Philippines so that the war against Hitler could be prosecuted first of all.

The new 4th Marines were going to Guam—that much they knew. Major General Roy S. Geiger had been given the job of taking Guam, using the 3rd Marine Division and the 1st Provisional Brigade. The old Raiders—the new 4th Marines—joined the new 22nd Marines to make up that brigade. Not much training was needed for the old Raiders; they had been trained to every infantry skill. Early in August 1944 they boarded assault ships and set sail for the Marianas. They thought they would be landing a few days after the landings were made on Saipan, but Saipan proved to be the toughest job yet for the Americans, and so the invasion of Guam was delayed for many weeks. The marines stayed aboard ship and waited. They were the "mobile reserve" that General Holland Smith thought he might have to use to crack the Japanese line at Saipan. So the ships cruised around during the last two weeks of June and the first weeks of July, most around Point Oak, a hundred miles off Saipan. Finally the ships began to run out of food, and so the 1st Brigade was taken back to Eniwetok and the marines had a chance to go ashore. But soon they were back aboard the LSTs and the destroyer transports, and heading for the northwest coast of Guam. The 4th Marines would land near Bangi Point, secure a beachhead, and then turn to attack the Orote Peninsula.

While the marines were at sea, for ten days the warships and aircraft bombarded Guam mercilessly. For three days navy underwater demolition teams worked over the Japanese shore defenses. Then came July 21, 1944, and the 1st Provisional Brigade began to land. The landing began at 6:30 A.M. Colonel Shapley's 4th Marines worked toward Mount Alifan. Tanks went after the pillboxes on the beach and just above it. The infantry concentrated on the snipers in the coconut trees. Then they went into a rice paddy, which the Japanese had covered with multiple fields of fire. The only way to get through was to infiltrate, a few men at a time. They did, and got up along a ridge line. They reorganized there, some 1,200 yards inland. From this point they were to make their way along a series of ridge lines, each defended stoutly by Japanese troops. By nightfall the 4th Marines had strung out along a thin line which extended 1,600 yards inland from the beach.

That night the marines established their perimeter. The Japanese came up in patrols after dark, and tried to draw fire, to force the marines to reveal their positions. They did so, and at midnight a mortar barrage worked over the seaward side of the 4th Marine position. It was followed by a banzai attack, with the Japanese using demolition charges and land mines. The Japanese charged in with samurai swords and bayonets, and six marines were stabbed in their foxholes that night. But the Japanese were turned back. An hour later they tried again, against Hill 40 only three hundred yards from the beach. The brunt of this attack was taken by Major Barney Green's 1st Battalion. The battalion was beaten down and forced to withdraw from its positions, but it reorganized at the base of Hill 40 and counterattacked. The marines took the hill. The Japanese came back and with superior force took it once more. Then a lieutenant came up with two squads, who crossed the rice paddy under fire and came to help the Green platoon. The troops reached the base of the hill again, and took the hill for the third time. This time it stayed in marine hands. The next morning more than four hundred dead Japanese troops were counted around Hill 40.

At 2:30 on the morning of D+1 the Japanese also counterattacked in the northwest, and again the 4th Marines took the brunt. This attack was led by Japanese tanks and gun trucks with the infantry in their wake. Once again it was a banzai attack, and the hills rang with the shouts and screams of the Japanese.

On came the tanks. A bazooka man from the 4th Marines stood up, firing his weapon, and knocked out three Japanese tanks before he was shot down. That action gave the marines a chance to bring a platoon of Sherman tanks up, which destroyed the other three Japanese tanks before they could move down the road. The loss of the armored point threw the Japanese into confusion; their plan had gone astray. Quickly they retreated behind Alifan.

But a second section of Japanese infantry, on the flank, kept on going after the main body stopped. The Japanese advance was covered by grenade throwers and machine guns. The Japanese came down a ravine, swinging swords and hurling grenades, led by an officer waving a bamboo pole with battle flag. The attackers were trying to head for the marine artillery positions, but they never got there. They were cut down by automatic fire from the old Raiders.

The third attack of this long night began at three A.M. The enemy had regrouped on a hill four hundred yards south of the marine lines. The 3rd Battalion (which had been the 3rd Battalion of the Raiders) was led then by Lieutenant Colonel Hoyler. He had the men ready in their foxholes, with stacks of grenades around them. At three the attack began, coming from the east, the Japanese rushing the foxholes and bayonetting the men inside. The attack was halted, but marine ammunition began to run low. The Japanese managed to infiltrate the artillery section and the artillery men had to fight as infantry to rout them. When morning came, some six hundred dead Japanese were counted on the 1st Brigade front. By nine A.M. the 4th Marines were advancing up the sides of Alifan, through pandanus clumps and prickly growth. They faced coconut log bunkers, which they blew up with grenades. They found Japanese fighting from caves, and threw in white phosphorus grenades, which created irritation and smoke to flush out the enemy. They climbed and they fought, leaving their packs behind. By nightfall they had captured Mount Alifan.

Once again on this second night the Japanese tried to infiltrate the lines. This time the marines had a remedy. They called for star shells from the destroyers offshore. The destroyers lit up the sky over Mount Alifan and the marines destroyed the enemy infiltrators with mortar and machine-gun fire.

On July 25 the marines were getting tired, but they continued their assault up the Orote Peninsula. The fighting was furious all along the route. On July 26, 1944, the marines were advancing along the Agat–Sumay road. But the Japanese were contesting every foot of ground, and the going was rough.

On July 27 this heavy fighting continued. Bullets were flying everywhere all day long. The marines advanced. The Japanese would not surrender, but they seemed resigned to defeat. At one point the marines watched forty Japanese in full battle gear come marching down the Sumay road, led by an officer carrying a battle flag. They came on in the face of tanks, machine guns, and rifles, and came on and on until every single Japanese had been shot down.

The marines reached the outskirts of Orote airfield, and here again found a new line of defense. At 8:30 on the morning of July 28 the attack began again. The 4th

Marines were west of the airfield, in thick jungle. The fighting was so fierce that three platoons lost their lieutenant platoon leaders in a few minutes, and in one platoon the leader, sergeant, guide, and two squad leaders fell. That sort of resistance was the lot of the 4th Marines all day long, but finally at four P.M. they broke through the enemy positions east of the airfield and killed the defenders. They had gone through some 250 pillboxes and gun emplacements.

The assault on Orote airfield, the principal Japanese airfield on Guam, began on the morning of July 29. Again it was the usual fight to the death for the enemy. On the west side the 4th Marines made progress, using flamethrowers against the installations. At one thick-walled tower they killed 125 Japanese. Some other Japanese escaped by running down to Santa Cruz and swimming through the harbor. That afternoon the marines captured the airfield and raised the United States flag above the wreckage of what had been the old U.S. Marine Corps barracks in the prewar days. And after that capture, the marines held a little ceremony on the island. Admiral Raymond Spruance and Lieutenant General Holland M. Smith came and the chaplains said prayers and there were speeches. It was all in celebration of the defense put up by the marines of the Guam garrison in 1941, when the area was overrun by the Japanese. A Japanese bugle was used to sound the colors, and then Old Glory was raised over the airfield. "On this hallowed ground," said Brigadier General Lemuel C. Shepherd, Jr., commander of the brigade, "you officers and men of the First Marine Brigade have avenged the loss of our comrades who were overcome by a numerically superior enemy five days after Pearl Harbor. Under our flag this island again stands ready to fulfill its destiny as an American fortress in the Pacific.''

Guam was really taken, but there was still much work to be done to mop up the Japanese defenders. For as the Americans came ever closer to the center of empire, the Japanese defenses became more determined. Mopping up continued until August 6, when the troops marched north through Agana to join the 3rd Marine Division in an attack designed to clear the whole island. By August 8 the Japanese were confined to the northernmost end of the island, hidden in caves or on wooded cliffs along the edges of the coast. On August 10 General Shepherd announced that the resistance was ended, but what he meant was the ability of the Japanese to carry a position. Snipers and skulkers continued to harry the marines for many weeks.

On August 22 troops began to leave the island. The army would take over the garrison duties. The 4th Marines went back to Guadalcanal, and there they were joined by the 29th Marines. The three regiments, 4th Marines, 22nd Marines, and 29th Marines, were then reassigned to the new 6th Marine Division with General Shepherd in command. And Colonel Shapley, the old Raider leader, received the Navy Cross for his leadership of the 4th Marines on Guam.

—24—
Okinawa

On March 15 the 6th Marine Division sailed for Okinawa. The trip was made in stages, with a stopover at Ulithi, the big new fleet base. The marines joined the invasion fleet there, and on March 27 sailed again, this time for the invasion which was to begin on April 1, Easter Sunday. The old Raiders, the 4th Marines, would head straight inland for Yontan airfield, whose capture was vital.

As the invasion fleet came in to Okinawa on Sunday morning, it was attacked by a number of Japanese aircraft, but none of them managed to drop bombs or strafe the ships, and all were shot down. American carrier planes also attacked the island's defenses that morning in a softening-up process. Then the men were over the side into landing craft and heading for the beach. The first wave hit the beach at 8:37 that morning. The 4th Marines landed on beaches Red 1, Red 2, and Red 3 and began pushing their way across the cane fields toward the airfield.

Just after landing, Major Barney Green's 1st Battalion rushed forward three hundred yards. The 3rd Battalion was scheduled to reach a line of old tombs, eight hundred yards from the beach, by evening, but actually Lieutenant Colonel Bruno Hochmuth's men got there early in the morning, meeting very little resistance. The Japanese had undergone a change of mind about their defenses. At first the commanders had planned to contest the invasion from the beaches onward, but later the plan had been changed and a whole system of interlocking caves and trenches near the shore had been deserted. This was a part of the changed defense plan that called for heavy use of kamikaze planes in waves, to strike at the invasion forces. The troops ashore would keep under cover for a while and then unleash a powerful counteroffensive, the Japanese had decided.

Therefore, the 4th Marines had no trouble at all in taking Yontan airfield although the high command had allocated three days for the capture of the field. It was deserted. They found bamboo poles camouflaged to look like antiaircraft guns, a number of wrecked aircraft that had been put back together again to make them look operational, and some dummy aircraft.

They did not see any Japanese on the field.

Nor did they see any Japanese on the field all day long. Then, that evening, while the marines were gathered around campfires, cooking their C rations, a Japanese fighter plane came in, circled the field, and landed. The pilot loosened the straps of his parachute seat, opened the canopy, and got out of the plane. He started walking toward the marines on the edge of the field, then suddenly realized that these were not Japanese troops and reached for the pistol at his hip. He never got it out of the holster, for he was riddled by bullets from several Garands.

"Well," said one marine, "there's always some S.O.B. that doesn't get the word, isn't there?"

By that time, equipment was being brought to the field, the Seabees were in action with bulldozers and loaders, and roads were being built around the airport. Before dark, three marine regiments were ashore, the 4th, 22nd, and 29th, and the vanguard of the 10th Army was on the other side of them.

On the second day, however, resistance stiffened. The 1st Battalion of the 4th Marines was caught in a ravine and pinned down by a superior Japanese force and had a desperate fight to get out, but did, killing perhaps a hundred and fifty Japanese in the process.

On the fourth day the 4th Marines advanced some more, holding the left flank of the 10th Army. They crossed the watershed at mid-island and moved down into the foothills on the opposite slope. They were working through very difficult terrain, sharp ridges and deep gullies full of trees and brush. They kept running up against small units of Japanese and finally learned that these were survivors of the battalion that had been occupying those caves and trenches near the shore, but had moved out before the landings. They moved fast, and within five days had reached the objectives they were supposed to attain in fifteen days. So the plans were changed, and the 4th Marines were given the task of advancing up the east coast of the

Ishikawa Isthmus. Patrols were sent ahead, and soon the 4th Marines assembled at Ora.

At the western tip of the Motobu Peninsula of Okinawa is a circle of coral ridges that from the air look like a giant volcanic crater. The ridges together form Mount Yaetake, 1,200 feet above sea level. Here the Japanese had built strong defenses, which controlled the Nago Toguchi and Itomi Toguchi roads. The terrain was very wisely selected by the Japanese, for it is so rugged that the marines could not use tanks or other mechanical equipment. Even infantry faced a difficult time.

The defending force of Japanese was organized around the 44th Independent Mixed Brigade, called the Udo force commanded by Colonel Udo. The Japanese had many weapons, from 150mm artillery down to machine guns and two 6.1-inch naval guns as well. In the center of the Mount Yaetake system, Colonel Udo had his command post in a cave that was connected to a whole system of defensive caves and trenches. All were linked by radio and telephone communication. Also, they had horses, which proved to be the best means of transport, and their defenses bristled with machine guns, mortars, and rifles. The 29th Marines began the assault on this powerful defense but soon brought the 4th Marines to the southwest coast of the peninsula to help. They decided on a coordinated attack on April 14.

That day the 4th Marines were assigned to seize a 700-foot-high ridge line about three-quarters of a mile inland from the coast. The 3rd Battalion moved out at 8:30 in the morning with the 2nd Battalion on the right and a battalion from the 29th Marines on the left.

The opposition was surprisingly light, and by noon

the objective had been seized. The 1st Battalion of the 4th Marines came up to protect the flank, but as the troops moved into the scrub pine of the coral cliffs, the opposition intensified. Machine guns opened up from concealed positions. Mortar fire began to rain down on the marines. The Japanese had obviously set up their weapons to cover all areas of approach very thoroughly. They would allow a squad or a whole platoon to cross an open space and then, when the next platoon thought the going was safe, they would open up on them, concentrating on officers and NCOs. It was dangerous to have a map, to carry a .45 pistol or a carbine instead of a Garand, or even to wave an arm as if directing someone. It was, said the marines, like fighting a phantom enemy. They did not see the Japanese, they saw only bullets and mortar rounds. The whole trail now became a trap. One platoon passed over this section of the trail without incident. But then along came the company commander with his headquarters company, and a machine gun mowed them down. Major Green was standing in his observation post when without warning a Nambu machine gun began firing and Major Green fell dead, three bullets in his body. Other marines swore that every Japanese must have a light Nambu machine gun. And still the Japanese were not seen.

By the end of that day, the 4th Marines had three battalions in the line. But nothing was going according to plan. The regimental weapons company was unable to use its weapons, so it was organized as an infantry company and fought in that manner. The hills ahead were full of Japanese, but no one knew quite where they were. One fire team, organized in the old Raider way, was sent on ahead, but was trapped by the

Japanese, who cut them off with machine-gun fire. From the rear came rescuers, but they had to employ smoke to rescue the wounded and get the rest of the team out of the gully in which they were trapped.

By nightfall Colonel Shapley was able to make an assessment of the situation. The enemy had two strong points. One was named Green Hill, not for Major Green, but for Lieutenant James H. Green, who was killed on the hill. There were two 75mm guns on that hill, and they were very well protected by Japanese infantry. The second strong point was at the summit of Mount Yaetake. Colonel Udo's forward elements were steadily withdrawing toward that position.

The next morning the 4th Marines began to drive forward again, three battalions abreast, with their objective two thirds of a mile away, the next ridge—the last ridge before Yaetake summit.

At noon the regiment had gotten halfway to its objective. On the left the 3rd Battalion was fighting for Green Hill. The 1st and 2nd Battalions were having plenty of trouble; the 2nd Battalion's Company G had sixty-five casualties, and three company commanders of the 2nd Battalion were evacuated as seriously wounded. The trouble came at Hill 200 even though that hill had been plastered by artillery fire and worked over by the guns of the battleship *Colorado*. But the Japanese had simply retreated during the bombardments to caves underground and stayed there until all was quiet, and then moved out to man their defenses. Hill 200 was taken twice that day and lost once, before the men of the 4th Marines could say it was safely held.

On the night of April 15 the 4th Marines halted their attack on Hill 200. Next day the attack would turn northward. Thus would the marines pinch Colonel Udo's defenders between the 4th Marines, the 29th Marines, and the 22nd Marines. In the battle for Green Hill the marines overran the summit the next morning and captured the two 75mm guns. Many Japanese died, sealed in the caves. And the next day Colonel Shapley launched the attack against Mount Yaetake.

The 1st Battalion's Company A, led by Captain Clinton B. Eastment, attacked on the left through the scrub pine. The company moved right along, meeting only some sporadic machine-gun fire. Company C, led by Lieutenant William H. Carlson, worked its way up a ravine. But from the top of the ridge behind, the officers of the 2nd Battalion could see that the Japanese were reinforcing the position with troops coming in from the west. So the battalion's 81mm mortars were unlimbered and they plastered the ridge line with shells. The Japanese activity on the ridge suddenly came to an end. The marines had fired 350 rounds of 81mm ammunition in two hours.

On the slope of Mount Yaetake the Japanese resisted stubbornly. Their commander was very smart. He held his fire until the marines of Company A reached the crest of the ridge, and then the Japanese defenders fired everything they had. The marines were driven back to the protection of an overhanging ledge. They brought out their 60mm mortars and began firing on the Japanese. The Japanese responded with knee mortars and grenades. Company A soon found its position untenable. They had to attack or retreat. But just then Lieutenant Carlson's Company C reached the summit of the ridge and could direct a crossfire on the Japanese. Under this cover Captain Eastment was able to advance up the slope and take his objective.

The fight for the summit of Mount Yaetake continued. The Japanese regrouped on the western slope of the mountain and prepared to attack again. But they were seen very clearly by the 2nd Battalion on Hill 200. So the 2nd Battalion laid down heavy mortar and machine-gun fire, and covered the reverse slope of the mountain with shelling, keeping the Japanese off balance and unable to try to rush the summit. Now other marines of the regiment came up to carry ammunition up to the 1st Battalion, which was running very short. Virtually everybody worked. A staff sergeant complained about carrying supplies. The man next to him picked up two boxes of machine-gun ammunition. He was a lieutenant. Colonel Beans, the old Raider, carried two water cans up to the front line. The other officers carried burdens, too. And when they came back they brought the wounded with them.

On the line of the 1st Battalion the troops were fending off a series of banzai attacks. The attacks continued all the rest of the day, for the Japanese knew that if they could not recapture Mount Yaetake, their major defense position was totally untenable. And by the end of the day the mountain was firmly in the hands of the marines of the 4th Regiment, and the Japanese on the mountain were reduced to the 347 bodies sprawled around the marine positions. General Shepherd came up to look over the battlefield. He was much impressed with what the marines had done, particularly since he saw how strong the Japanese positions had been. It was the stoutest defense he had yet seen, and an indication of what the marines would face in future assaults, as, perhaps, on Japan itself. But here on Okinawa the Japanese were still far from finished, and even on the Motobu Peninsula there was another major Japanese defense position on the Itomi-Toguchi road. Also, there was word from intelligence that about a thousand Japanese had escaped and were now going to try to break out of the peninsula into northern Okinawa.

—— 25 ——

Battle of Naha

On April 19 the old Raiders of the new 4th U.S. Marines attacked along the Itomi-Toguchi road on Okinawa. The resistance was very light, although the system of defenses that the Japanese had built in this area was impressive. In the change of tactics they had abandoned the system. On April 24 scouts saw a large band—probably three hundred—of Japanese near Kawada on the east coast. Two companies moved to intercept. They engaged the enemy and killed a hundred and fifty of them.

This was a sort of mopping-up operation, but the numbers to be mopped up in the area were still quite large, and the mopping up was fairly costly. As far as the whole 6th Marine Division was concerned, in the last ten days of April they killed 2,500 Japanese and took 46 prisoners with a loss of 236 men killed and 1,061 wounded.

By the beginning of May the Japanese defense plan was obvious. General Ushijima, the Japanese commander, knew that there was no hope of winning the battle for Okinawa because the Americans had so much more materiel and so many more men to put into the fight. But he had been instructed to fight to the death and to make victory as difficult as possible for the Americans, and that was precisely what he was doing.

The key to Ushijima's defense was the Naha-Shuri line. To help with the assault the 4th Marines and the rest of the 6th Division were moved down early in April to the Chibana area. Soon they found themselves immersed in mud so thick that bulldozers had to be used to get the trucks out of the mire, and sometimes the bulldozers bogged down.

The 4th Marines were in reserve until May 19, when they relieved the 29th Marines on Sugar Loaf Hill, one of the key points in the Japanese defense line. The Japanese were well ensconced in caves and tunnels throughout the area, defenses that had been prepared with great care and were used with great perspicacity. As the 4th Marines moved up in relief, they took a serious shelling from Japanese guns. When it was over, Lieutenant Colonel Hochmuth's 3rd Battalion had suffered 40 casualties. In all, during ten days of fighting for Sugar Loaf Hill the 6th Marine Division had taken more than 2,600 casualties. The Japanese were tough, no doubt about it. But so were the marines. One marine was bayoneted by a Japanese soldier in the right shoulder, right arm, and neck. The Japanese drew back for another thrust, and the marine jammed his knee into the man's stomach, then leapt on him, clamped his arm around the soldier's neck, and strangled him to death.

Another marine found a Japanese knee mortar in a cave and carried it to his foxhole. He used it to fend off a Japanese attack.

Another marine missed death four times in one day. A shell landed so close that shrapnel ripped up his pack. Another shell landed less than fifty yards from him, but he was unhit. Later that day machine-gun bullets tore off his cartridge belt. That night a Japanese soldier crept up to his foxhole and tried to bayonet him. The marine grabbed the Japanese by the back of his neck and stabbed him to death with his trench knife.

One lieutenant heard a man talking and warned him that if he did not stop he might bring the Japanese onto them. The man said something inaudible. The next thing the lieutenant heard was the sound of a grenade banging against a helmet. He realized that only a Japanese grenade was so armed, and as the grenade came into his foxhole the lieutenant came out, rifle in hand, and shot down the Japanese.

Once Sugar Loaf Hill was captured, the men of the 4th Marines could look down across the Asato River on Naha, the capital city of Okinawa, or what remained of it. Naha had been blasted into rubble by this time. The Japanese defenses were still intact, under ground, and in the ruined buildings.

On May 19 the 4th Marines moved up to Naha. The Japanese artillery in the Shuri Hills pounded them as they came, and the men were forced to lie prone and dig their foxholes. The casualties numbered seventy, but by 2:30 that afternoon the 4th Marines were in place.

At eight A.M. on May 20 they attacked toward the river, with two battalions abreast. The 2nd Battalion got up onto Half Moon Hill, which dominated the area known as the Horseshoe. The 3rd Battalion made it up onto King Hill, which looked down on the Horseshoe from the other side. All this while they were under fire from artillery in the Shuri Hills. They dug in that afternoon and waited.

At 9:30 that night the Japanese made a very strong counterattack. This was no banzai charge, but a battalion attack preceded by a heavy mortar barrage, and most of the pressure was directed against the 3rd Battalion on the right. The marines countered with a barrage laid down by six battalions of artillery, the shells placed just before the lines of the 3rd Battalion. But the Japanese kept coming, until Colonel Shapley had to commit part of his reserves to this sector to be sure of holding. The 3rd Battalion did hold, and the next day the marines counted more than five hundred dead Japanese soldiers in front of their positions.

The rains came then, rains that lasted for nine days. On the morning of May 22 the 1st and 3rd Battalions of the 4th Marines drove toward the Asato River, in the rain. The mud became so soupy that trucks could not move, so the supplies for the men had to be brought up by amphibious tractor.

Patrols were sent to cross the river and find out the situation of the Japanese on the far bank.

Two patrols crossed the stream and penetrated about two hundred yards into the ruins of the town of Machishi. They came under machine-gun fire on three sides, and returned to report that the enemy had many weapons here.

Later in the morning more patrols were sent out to the river, and across, and at noon in heavy rain the regiment set out to attack across the stream. The object of the attack was a long ridge that came out from Naha. It was laced with caves full of Japanese soldiers with plenty of arms and ammunition. The fire was intense as the Americans crossed, but by 1:30 the leading elements of two battalions were across and they had driven into the Japanese lines some three hundred yards.

The going was extremely difficult. The banks were steep, the mud was thick, and so was the Japanese fire. The marines tried to bring up tanks and tank destroyers, but these vehicles bogged down in the mire. Food and ammunition had to go across the river by manpower. The engineers tried to bridge the stream, but the Japanese fire was too withering. It was infantry all the way, marines inching forward, always under fire. Still, by nightfall they had moved five hundred yards past the stream and into the eastern suburbs of Naha.

As night fell, Lieutenant Henry Herz's platoon of engineers came up with an idea for bridging the stream. They would run five amtracs into the water and sink them to be used as piers for the bridge. They tried. But two of the amtracs were destroyed by land mines before they could be put in place. That was an indication of how many mines there were in this area. Two more amtracs were brought up, and the engineers hand-carried the one-hundred-pound sections of prefabricated footbridge and finally got them in place to form two bridges across the river. These were foot-bridges only wide enough for a single infantryman to cross with stanchions and rope on one side. Once they were in place, the engineers began work on a Bailey bridge, which would be capable of taking vehicles. As morning came, so did the Japanese shelling, but the engineers continued to work under fire, and by mid-afternoon they had the Bailey bridge in place, and tanks could cross the river.

Meanwhile the two battalions of the 4th Marines moved forward, but at an agonizingly slow pace. The mud was the worst problem. On the evening of May 25 the marines held most of the north-south ridge west of Machishi. That night the Japanese counterattacked the 1st Battalion, as expected. The marines were ready. After forty-five minutes of fighting the Japanese fell back.

That night the division reconnaissance company moved out in front, into Naha, and secured positions. The next day the company moved into the center of Naha. The 4th Marines did not go so fast. They had to clear mines and secure the city, step by step, street by street. On May 27 and May 28 it rained again, so hard that no progress could be made, and on May 29 the 4th Marines were relieved by the 29th Marines, and went into reserve. They had been fighting steadily for nine days, in mud, mud, mud. The weathermen said that during that period eighteen inches of rain had fallen. Mud and mines and mortar fire plus artillery had cost the old Raider regiment 1,100 casualties in those nine days, but they had killed twice as many Japanese soldiers, and they had cracked the main

242

Japanese defense line. The Japanese were moving back all across the island.

The most important objective after Naha was its airfield, for the high ground commanded control of the Naha harbor and threatened the American drive to the southern part of the island. Japanese guns on this high ground faced seaward, and they could fire on any amphibious invaders.

Admiral Minoru Ota, the commander of Japanese naval defenses, was convinced that the marines would continue to drive eastward overland, and would assult the Orote Peninsula from the base. The admiral knew his enemies, the Marine Raiders, whom he had first met at New Georgia. He was sure the marines would drive up from the base of the Orote Peninsula overland, so he put his infantry into place facing the base of the peninsula and sited his guns to fire inland.

But General Shepherd decided to make an amphibious landing, and so the 4th Marines came out of reserve to lead the assault with tanks, after which the 29th Marines would follow.

On the afternoon of June 3, the tanks were put aboard LCTs and the next morning infantrymen went aboard LVTs and were taken south along the reef. Warships offshore began plastering the landing area with high explosive. In the hour before 5:45 A.M. they poured 4,300 rounds of everything from 75mm ammunition to fourteen-inch shells into the beach. At 5:47 the men of the 4th Marines went into the beach with the tanks right behind them.

The bombardment had helped, but it was apparent that the Japanese had been surprised because Japanese opposition on the beach was minimal and the 2nd

Battalion moved forward under only sporadic machine-gun fire and assaulted the ridge above the landing area.

The Japanese were still suffering from the surprise as the 4th Marines began to drive inland, and the 29th Marines began landing. They moved up the rising hills behind the beach. They passed well-prepared positions that had been built months, years earlier, but were now abandoned. By mid-afternoon Admiral Ota was moving his troops, and the defense line began to stiffen. The fire from automatic weapons was very heavy, for the Japanese were using antiaircraft guns and even machine guns taken from crashed aircraft in their defense pattern. The marines encountered many mines in the mud this day, and mine removal was the biggest problem they faced—mines and the mud. By the end of the day they held about half the airfield, and a line that extended about a mile from the beach.

The night of June 4 was marked by almost constant mortaring of the marine line by the enemy. On the morning of June 5 the 4th Marines moved again, at 7:30, slowly against strong Japanese fire, but steadily until around noon, when the 3rd Battalion was stopped by a strong Japanese position at the village of Toma, in the center of the peninsula, just below the airfield. Tanks were brought up, and helped some, but by the end of the day the marine line ran from the village of Omine on the coast, down past the end of the airfield, through the lower edge of Toma and to the Kokoba Estuary below Onoyama Island.

That night the engineers made real progress: they put up a pontoon bridge that crossed the Kokoba

Estuary and gave the marines direct contact with Naha and their supply line.

Now the marines came up against the core of the Japanese defense in this area, along the ridge that runs northwest-southeast, parallel to the Kokoba Estuary. The advance in this area was practically nil on June 6. Only the right side of the 4th Marine line advanced, almost to Gushi down by the coast. But at the end of that day, the whole airfield was in marine hands. Division sent officers up to see why the advance was so slow, and they went back to report the reason: the Japanese defenses on Orote Peninsula, they said, were stronger than those the Americans had defended for weeks on Corregidor in the Philippines.

The marines spent the day blasting the mouths of caves to seal them up. Two marines entered one cave, expecting to find a machine gun, perhaps. But they went back a hundred and fifty yards inside the hill. There they killed one Japanese soldier, but he was the only one they saw. Then they stopped and looked in awe at what they had stumbled on: a whole system of winding corridors with sleeping quarters for enlisted men and private rooms for officers, three floors of apartments, connected by ladders, enough space and enough equipment to house a battalion. The corridors were lighted by a power system that ran back to the central grid in Naha. The officers' rooms even had overstuffed chairs and beds. Down in the bottom level were supplies, food, ammunition, medical supplies, a switchboard, and radio equipment.

On June 6 the 4th Marines ran into very strong opposition at Gushi. The major obstacle was a tight defense position on Hill 57. Colonel Shapley decided on an attack by his 2nd and 3rd Battalions. At noon three platoons of tanks came up to support the assault, and the tanks moved forward. By dark the infantry had carried the hill with the help of the tanks, and a hundred Japanese defenders had been killed.

On June 7 the 4th Marines attacked more of the high ground south of Uibaru. They fought all day and captured the little town. But the hills in this area were steep and infested with enemy troops and Hill 38, near Uibaru, stoutly resisted. Finally the 2nd Battalion of the 4th Marines moved through the Japanese system of underground tunnels to break out on the hill and attack the Japanese from the reverse slope. This maneuver was so successful that they tried it on another hill and it worked too.

On June 10 the 4th Marines moved forward again, but that night they were counterattacked by the Japanese. The heavy blows fell on the 1st Battalion, and the fighting lasted almost all night. Next morning the marines counted two hundred dead Japanese soldiers around their positions.

The fighting in this area continued until June 13, when the whole peninsula finally fell into marine hands. The Oroku victory was costly, 1,600 marines had been killed or wounded. But they found the bodies of Admiral Ota and his entire staff, suicides all—and they counted some 5,000 dead Japanese soldiers and sailors, and 200 prisoners of war.

At the end a number of Japanese surrendered when they saw that the battle was really over, and more prisoners were taken on Okinawa than before; it was a sign of the growing Japanese disillusion with the war. And then it was on again, not to reserve but on to the south to the Mezado Ridge on the right flank of the U.S. 10th Army.

The battle for Okinawa continued.

—26—
End of the Line

June 18, 1945. Kuwanga Ridge, north of Kiyamu, was one of the highly fortified positions of the Japanese defenders in the southern end of Okinawa. It was attacked first by the 22nd Marines, but they had been fighting hard for weeks, and their ranks were depleted. So the 4th Marines were brought up as soon as the ridge line was captured. The 4th Marines could look down and see the ocean beyond Kiyamu Ridge, and they knew that the battle for Okinawa was coming to its end. Soon the Japanese would have nowhere to go but into the sea.

But there was still much bloody fighting to be done, for the vast majority of the Japanese troops had no thought of surrender, even though they knew that the battle for Okinawa was all but lost.

On the morning of June 19 the 1st and 3rd Battalions of the 4th Marines opened their assault against Kiyamu Ridge. The place chosen was Ibaru Ridge, a strongly defended spot. The attackers pushed hard, and by evening had corraled the Japanese in an area five thousand yards square. The next day ought to tell the end of the story.

The 4th Marines faced Kiyamu Ridge squarely. The trouble was that the north face, at which they looked, was so precipitous that no one could attack there. They would have to attack from the rear, they knew. Then, with the sight of the water, some Japanese had second thoughts about dying for the emperor. That afternoon seven hundred Japanese soldiers chose mass surrender. Theirs was the greatest surrender in the Pacific war. Another forty climbed down to a ledge just above the sea and blew themselves up with grenades. Other Japanese in caves killed themselves thus, and some of them also killed civilians who would have liked nothing better than to surrender. Marines who spoke Japanese used loudspeakers to broadcast to the Japanese, and this time the broadcasts had results. By the end of June 20 some two thousand Japanese soldiers had surrendered. More kept coming all the time, and the next day, after eighty-two days of fighting, the war on Okinawa ended. The American flag was unfurled over a little knoll at the southern tip of the island. Okinawa was captured. The island was secured.

The fighting ended, it was time for medals of recognition for the brave. One such was the Medal of Honor awarded to Corporal Richard E. Bush, a squad leader with Company C of the 4th Marines. Corporal Bush won his medal at Mount Yaetake, in the grim fight for that rocky crag. He had led his squad and inspired them with determination, and then he was wounded.

With other wounded men he was evacuated to a safe position behind the rocks of the lower part of the position. But a Japanese on the other side of the rocks hurled a hand grenade into the area where the wounded were being treated. Corporal Bush pulled the grenade to him and shielded it with his hand and body to protect other men. He was wounded again, and he lost three fingers, but he survived.

PFC Anthony E. Borgia won the Navy Cross for heroism in a battle on the Oroku Peninsula. He was operating a flamethrower when it ran out of fuel. Just then thirty-seven Japanese rushed the position. PFC Borgia was armed now with only a .45-caliber pistol, but he began firing it. He killed one Japanese soldier, seized his rifle, and began firing it at the others. He fired with such determination and accuracy that he scattered the enemy, and other marines came up and finished the job.

Another Navy Cross was awarded to Corporal Hugh A. Vogel, chief of a 37mm antitank platoon of the old 2nd Raider Battalion, now the weapons company of the 4th Marines. He was directing fire for his platoon when he came upon a Japanese squad operating a 13mm gun. He killed the crew, captured the gun, and turned it on the Japanese, destroying a mortar that was harassing his men. That same night he attacked two Japanese-held caves with demolition charges and sealed them up.

Lieutenant Colonel Fred D. Beans, executive officer of the 4th Marines and former commander of the 3rd Raider Battalion, was awarded the Silver Star after he took over one battalion during the fight for Mount Yaetake. The commander of the battalion had been killed, and many men wounded in the vigorous fighting for the mountain. Colonel Beans reorganized the battalion and led it to win an important position.

Lieutenant Howard A. Berrian also won a Silver Star when he took over a rifle platoon at the height of a battle. His job was command of a 60mm mortar platoon with the 3rd Battalion, but he did not hesitate to lead the rifle platoon out to attack the Japanese. He also supervised the evacuation of several wounded men who were at the base of a cliff by tying ropes around them so they could be lifted out of the dangerous position.

Corporal Dennis J. Hines, a fire team leader with Company B of the 1st Battalion of the 4th Marines, won a Silver Star on Sugar Loaf Hill. He was wounded in the foot, but within an hour returned to action and led his fire team against half a dozen Japanese-held caves. He was wounded again, but refused to be evacuated until the company's objectives had been reached.

PFC John L. MacDonald of Company B was pinned down, along with his fire team, while assaulting a Japanese hill. He led the fire team around the Japanese flank, ran to within ten feet of the enemy position, and with grenades and rifle killed eight Japanese. When his platoon was ordered to withdraw, he covered the other men until the last one was out safe, and then went back himself. For this he won the Silver Star.

Lieutenant Marion E. Price's Company A got into trouble on Kiyamu Ridge; he volunteered to go with the company commander and two other marines on a reconnaissance mission. The party was ambushed by the Japanese. Lieutenant Price picked up a BAR and covered the others. Then he saw that the company commander was wounded and that the others could not drag him to safety, so Lieutenant Price moved up to where the commander was lying and began firing from that position, only a dozen yards from the enemy, and forced them to keep their heads down. He did this for an hour, and then when help arrived Lieutenant Price helped carry the captain to safety. He won the Silver Star.

Corporal Duey C. Thompson of Company A was fighting on Hill 58 on the Oroku Peninsula when he saw an enemy mortar firing on other marines from a small cave on the forward slope of the hill. Under enemy fire he made five trips down the hill and each time threw a grenade into the cave. Still the enemy kept firing that mortar. Then Corporal Thompson prepared a demolition charge, ran down to the lip of the cave, and dropped the charge into the entrance. The explosion sealed up the cave. The mortar did not fire again, and Corporal Thompson won the Silver Star.

These were the medals. But for every medal winner there were ten acts of heroism that went unrewarded. For the total, the men of the old Raider regiments, and now of the 4th Marines, won a Presidential Unit citation for their fighting on Okinawa. A hundred and one days after that fight began, they left Naha aboard transports bound for Guam and a rest in surroundings that seemed sheer luxury. They had a Red Cross canteen, with Red Cross hostesses—real live American girls. They had USO shows and movies every night. And there were hundreds of Bronze Stars and other medals to remind Americans of the heroism of these marines. Colonel Beans took over the regiment as commander. It would be his job to get the old

Raiders ready for their coming task, the attack on the Japanese mainland near Tokyo.

Then came August 1945, and the Japanese surrender, and on that day the 4th Marines left for Japan to become part of the occupation army. They joined the ships of Admiral Halsey's 3rd Fleet and sailed for Yokosuka, the big Japanese naval base not far from Tokyo. On the morning of August 30 Major Frank Carney led the 2nd Battalion ashore, the first foreign invaders ever to set foot on Japanese soil. There was no resistance and no violence. On September 6 the 4th Marines took over the base area. A few days later 120 men of the old 4th Marines, who had been prisoners of war since the surrender on Corregidor, came down to visit the new outfit.

The old Raiders remained on duty in Japan for several months, but in April 1946 the entire 6th Marine Division was deactivated, and the Raiders who were still left abroad became a part of the 3rd Marine Brigade.

The Raider concept was apparently unlamented at the time by many officers of the Marine Corps. But the idea of a special force of highly trained fighting men to do the tough jobs was not really dead. It emerged once more during the Vietnam War when it became obvious that specialists of this sort would be needed, and the army's Green Berets and the marine force recon units were utilized.

And the old Raiders, now mostly returned to civil life, could recall with pride the accomplishments of their battalions at Makin, Guadalcanal, New Georgia, Guam, and Okinawa. The 1st Raider Battalion in particular had saved the day on Bloody Ridge above Henderson Field, when the Japanese swarmed down in those early days of the fighting. And all the rest of the way the men of the Raider battalions had performed with courage and military efficiency.

In the fall of 1944 the Marine Corps had changed its collective mind about the need for such special units, and although Admiral Richmond Kelly Turner and some others advocated the formation of a Raider division, and at least the development of a Raider battalion for every other division, it was not to come to pass. The two provisional regiments of Raiders had been dissolved and the men reassigned. Evans Carlson, who had originated the gung-ho concept that so worried so many professional naval and marine officers because it was at variance with their ideas of discipline, had gone to Saipan as planning officer on the staff of General Harry Schmidt. He had been wounded there, and that had put an end to his active marine career. After the war he kept in touch with some of his old Raiders. He started to go into politics, but a heart attack put a premature end to his life.

Carlson had brought the gung-ho concept from China; Colonel Shapley had knocked it out when he took over the battalion; Joe McCaffery had revived the idea on Bougainville, and Major Washburn had kept it going because he was one of the originals of the Raiders. But when they became the 4th Marines, much of that attitude was lost, and in the heavy fighting on

Guam and Okinawa many of the original Raiders were casualties.

So the Raiders passed into the pages of history, but they and their deeds would not be forgotten wherever brave men congregated to tell of the exploits of the marines in the great Pacific war.